Understanding
Anxiety
& Panic Attacks

Professor Kwame McKenzie

Published by Family Doctor Publications Limited
in association with the British Medical Association

IMPORTANT
This book is intended not as a substitute for personal
medical advice but as a supplement to that advice for
the patient who wishes to understand more about his
or her condition.

Before taking any form of treatment
YOU SHOULD ALWAYS CONSULT YOUR MEDICAL
PRACTITIONER.

In particular (without limit) you should note that
advances in medical science occur rapidly and some
information about drugs and treatment contained in this
booklet may very soon be out of date.

Family Doctor Publications, PO Box 4664, Poole, Dorset BH15 1NN

ISBN-13: 978 1 903474 136
ISBN-10: 1 903474 13 2

20062010

Contents

About the author

Kwame McKenzie is Professor of Psychiatry at the University of Toronto and Senior Psychiatrist at the Centre for Addictions and Mental Health. He has worked at all levels from clinical care to writing government policy. He is committed to improving the understanding of mental illness and has written over 100 academic articles and 4 books, hosted a TV series and conducted numerous radio interviews on the subject.

Introduction

What is anxiety?

It is almost impossible to live without anxiety or fear. It is widespread. We feel anxious regularly, although for each of us different events, situations or relationships will make us feel anxious. Lots of things make us anxious or fearful, from everyday events such as crossing the road or meeting new people to bigger decisions such as which school our children should go to or whether or not we should visit the doctor because we develop a pain. Anxiety affects everybody at times.

Anxiety and fear

There is a subtle difference between anxiety and fear. Fear is the feeling that you have when you see or experience something that frightens you. Anxiety can be regarded as a type of fear that you experience when you are thinking or worrying about something rather than actually experiencing it.

I may fear for my life if a car speeds towards me when I am in the middle of the road but if I am sitting in my house, thinking about and becoming concerned about safety on the roads, I could be described as being anxious about it. Anxiety and fear lead to similar feelings in the body.

Fear is an important defence mechanism that has always been with us. People who do not feel fear can be dangerous to themselves and it can be dangerous to be with them.

Some scientists believe that fear has an evolutionary basis. There are some objects that we are programmed to be scared of. These basic fears include certain animals such as snakes and spiders. As we were evolving, individuals with well-honed fear responses to these animals would have been more likely to survive and they would have been more likely to have had children and passed their genes on to the next generation. It takes millions of years for evolution to catch up and so some of our current fears may be linked to survival mechanisms from a long time ago.

Fear is both physical and psychological. Situations that provoke fear cause a release of hormones and chemicals that change our body functions. These responses were set up for past times when life was less sophisticated and our challenges were more obvious. The hormones and chemicals cause changes in the body that keep us alert, make us steel ourselves perhaps to fight or prepare us to run away.

We saw a predator, we recognised that it could be a danger to us and so we needed to prepare ourselves to fight it or to run away. Alternatively, we saw a possible source of food, perhaps a gazelle, which we did not want to miss the chance of catching because we needed to eat. We needed to think quickly, we needed to be ready to run and catch it, we needed to change our body state so that our performance was optimal.

Catching prey or fighting for our lives requires only short-lived changes in our body physiology. After we have escaped or after the kill there is no need for our bodies to burn excess energy and so it returns to normal.

Our fear responses work well for these sorts of short-lived situations. Our bodies at this time are focused on one thing that is more important than anything else we need to do. When the problem has passed we return to normal and continue with everyday life.

Our fear response is set up to deal with severe short-lived physical problems with which our bodies need to deal.

Fear and anxiety in the modern world

The world has changed, however. Our worries and anxieties now are often not about physical threats or short-term problems. For instance, they may be about the future and how we are going to cope with problems or about situations that may arise but have not yet done so. Anxiety comes from the Latin *anxius,* which means to worry about an uncertain event.

Our bodies use the same set of responses for anxiety as they use for fear. The problem is that our fear response is built to deal with sudden obvious danger but it does not work well for uncertain events. It does not know when best to switch on or turn off. If our fear response is maintained for too long, we feel panicky and uncomfortable. We find it difficult to continue with our day-to-day lives.

We are set up to deal with short-lived physical challenges but the threats we come across are often diffuse, may last some time and are psychological rather than physical. The threats are not in front of us. They are often situations that we cannot necessarily control. You cannot run away from rising debts, for example. It is impossible to fight job uncertainty physically. Nevertheless, these situations are important threats to our way of life.

We are left with a prehistoric defence mechanism in the twenty-first century. Our bodies are built to deal with short-lived fears, but our world produces longer-term worries.

The two are not a good match and, not surprisingly, the mismatch makes us prone to anxiety problems. The fact that more people do not suffer from such problems is the result of the fact that humans have an amazing ability to adapt. We all find ways of dealing with the stresses of our complex lives, but stresses and coping are finely balanced.

This book should help you to understand anxiety problems. You can think of an anxiety problem as fear or anxiety that either lasts too long or is too great compared with the threat. As a result, it causes problems in everyday life.

Challenging or threatening situations produce anxiety and sometimes fear. This is a normal reaction that is vital for survival.

But if the fear or anxiety is severe, persistent or out of proportion to the threat, or if it impairs your everyday life and your work, you probably have an anxiety disorder.

The good news is that anxiety disorders can usually be treated effectively, often without medication.

This book helps you understand what is happening to you and what treatments are on offer. It is not a therapy book that you can use by itself, but it will be a useful reference before and during the treatment that you receive from your GP, therapist or specialist.

KEY POINTS

- It is almost impossible to live without anxiety or fear

- Anxiety can be regarded as a type of fear that you experience when you are thinking or worrying about something rather than actually experiencing it

- Our bodies are built to deal with short-lived fears, but our world produces longer-term worries

- An anxiety problem is a fear or anxiety that either lasts too long or is out of proportion compared with the threat

- Anxiety disorders can usually be treated effectively, often without medication

Causes of anxiety and fear

What causes anxiety and fear?

Anxiety and fear are often caused by stress. Anxiety and fear are the feelings that we experience when we are cornered and we feel threatened. However, we do not always know exactly why we feel threatened.

We all have minor fears. We are taught some of them; others seem to be innate (instinctive). Babies start off being happy to be held by anyone, but after a few months they become afraid of strangers and often cry if they are picked up by people who are unfamiliar to them. You can understand how this could work to their benefit. Childbirth used to be dangerous and mothers often died. A baby who was not happy to be picked up by any adult soon after birth would find it difficult to attract someone to look after him or her if the mother died or was sick. However, after a few months of being well looked after, it would be important to stay with and be protected by the person who was familiar and trusted. Strangers would be a threat to the baby's existence and because of this they call out when strangers come near them.

Other fears also seem to be genetic, such as our fears of animals that scurry about, or fears of snakes or of heights. We can all think of plausible explanations why we may be scared of them, for instance they may pass on germs that could kill us, they could bite us, or we may fear falling and hurting ourselves.

Some facts, however, just do not fit. There are very few people who are afraid of cars – although they are one of the most important causes of accidents in the UK. And there are lots of people who are afraid of flying in planes, although they are very safe indeed. This is what makes people think that we are predisposed to fearing some situations but not others.

Anxiety and performance

It is normal to be fearful. A little fear is good for us. A little bit of anxiety sharpens up our game. It puts us a bit on edge and improves our performance. A little bit of fear helps us to think quickly, and it makes us work better physically. Students who are not anxious do less well in exams and people who are not appropriately anxious in interviews do not do as well. In extreme situations, those who are fearful think and act quicker and so are more likely to survive than those who are fearless. Fear responses have their place.

However, extreme fear and anxiety are not at all good for us. They impede our performance. Some people become so worried before public speaking that they sweat and stutter over their lines. Some students become so anxious over their exams that they cannot prepare properly for them; every time they sit down they worry about how they will do. Some people do badly in interviews because they are too nervous and some people become so fearful in extreme situations that they totally freeze.

There is a trade-off between a person's level of anxiety and his or her performance. Mental and physical performance increases as the level of anxiety increases but gradually reaches a point where for every increase in level of anxiety performance decreases – and decreases quickly. We all need some fear, but too much and we just cannot perform.

If you are too relaxed you may not perform well. If you are over-anxious or over-stressed your performance deteriorates.

Anxiety can cause further anxiety

There is a further problem: anxiety and stress can produce a vicious circle. For instance, exam students who have become too anxious and cannot revise because they are worrying about how well they are going to do may soon realise that they have not been working.

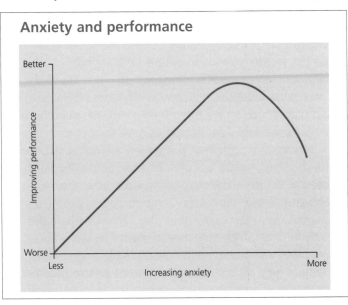

Anxiety and performance

This will make them more worried and produce more anxiety and more time wasted about how they are going to fare. The more they worry, the less time they spend working and the more they worry.

There are other forms of anxiety that are not helpful. Later in the book forms of anxiety are described that seem to have no reason and are unrelated to any event. In addition fears and anxieties are described that are extreme compared with the threat. These forms of anxiety have no useful function at all and can be distressing.

Sometimes the timing of our anxiety goes awry. During a traumatic event some people seem to cope very well but hours or even days later their anxiety kicks in. This sort of delayed fear and anxiety response is, again, very distressing and not useful.

How common are anxiety problems?

Anxiety is an everyday event for many people. Anxiety that causes problems with our enjoyment of life affects a lot of people. It is estimated that 14 per cent of the population (14 in every 100) have a problem that could benefit from treatment. Anxiety problems are very common and they are the most common psychological problem in the UK. They are more common than depression. Anxiety can become an escalating vicious circle, whereby the existence of anxiety produces other effects in the body, such as physical symptoms, that cause even more anxiety.

Does my anxiety need treatment?

The simple answer is that, if your anxiety affects the way in which you live and if it affects your enjoyment of life, you may benefit from treatment. But, beware,

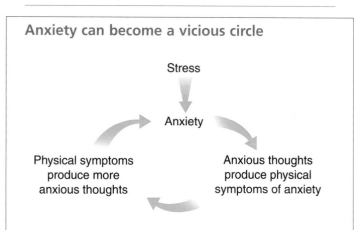

Anxiety can become a vicious circle

Stress

Anxiety

Physical symptoms produce more anxious thoughts

Anxious thoughts produce physical symptoms of anxiety

the drive that some people have to succeed is based on their anxieties about themselves. So, if you were to try to get rid of anxiety altogether, you could feel more relaxed but you could diminish your drive to succeed.

How common is anxiety?

Type of anxiety	Percentage of adults (aged 16–64) with anxiety problems	
Mixed anxiety and depression	8 per cent	(8 in 100)
Generalised anxiety	3 per cent	(3 in 100)
Obsessive–compulsive	1 per cent	(1 in 100)
Panic disorder	1 per cent	(1 in 100)
Phobias	1 per cent	(1 in 100)
Total	**14 per cent**	**(14 in 100)**

KEY POINTS

- Anxiety and fear are normal reactions that we need so that we can respond properly to threats

- Too much anxiety stops us performing properly

- Anxiety disorders are the result of too much or inappropriate anxiety

- Fourteen per cent of the population at some time suffer from anxiety problems that could be treated

- If your anxiety affects the way that you live your life, consider getting treatment

Symptoms of anxiety

The fight, flight or fright response

Our fear response is set up for dealing with a physical threat or opportunity. Some people call it a fight, flight or fright response because those seem to be the options that our body is giving us – we freeze, fight our foe or run away.

Our body gets ready for action in a number of ways. A number of hormones are released into our bloodstream from the glands in which they are stored. They have effects on our nerves and other organs, preparing us for action.

The chief hormone is adrenaline (also known as epinephrine). It causes our heart to beat quicker, makes our blood pressure go up and gets us to breathe quicker. These actions make sure that we have lots of blood full of oxygen so that the muscles can work effectively.

Adrenaline helps to make sure that our body uses this blood efficiently. It makes some blood vessels bigger and others smaller, and in this way causes blood to be diverted to the parts of the body that most need it.

The muscles in our legs and arms are needed for fighting or running away and so they receive preferential treatment. The brain is provided with extra blood so that we stay alert and can think about what we need to do. Less important functions, such as digesting food, are put on the back burner, so blood to the stomach is decreased. Blood to the skin is also decreased.

If we need to run, however, we need to run fast. Hence we need to be as light as we can. Adrenaline affects the muscles in our bladder and bowel. Being as light as we can be could be the difference between getting away and being caught. Adrenaline makes us feel like urinating and defecating so that we can get rid of excess water and solids.

If we are running and using extra energy we do not want to overheat. Hence our bodies sweat. The water cools us off. Adrenaline also gives our sensory organs a pep up. We become tense so that everything can act and react more quickly.

These bodily changes correspond to the symptoms that we feel when we are anxious, for instance:

- We feel our heart pounding or feel like we have palpitations because adrenaline has pushed our heart rate up.

- We feel dizzy because adrenaline has changed our blood pressure.

- We may feel a little short of breath because we are breathing faster.

- We get butterflies in the stomach because the blood is diverted from here and we may feel like going to the toilet because the muscles to the bladder are affected.

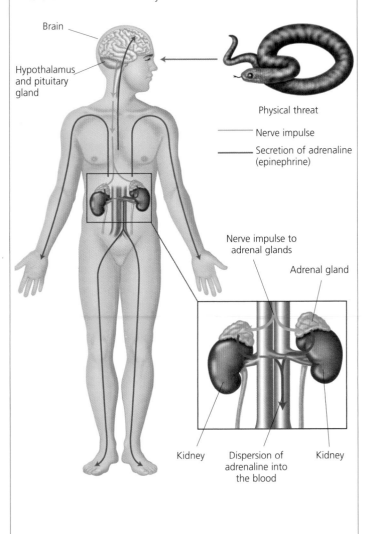

Adrenaline and the fear response

Adrenaline is released in the body in response to a physical threat or opportunity. It has a variety of effects within the body to ensure that we are ready to deal with the situation.

Brain

Hypothalamus and pituitary gland

Physical threat

Nerve impulse

Secretion of adrenaline (epinephrine)

Nerve impulse to adrenal glands

Adrenal gland

Kidney

Dispersion of adrenaline into the blood

Kidney

What are the symptoms of anxiety?

There are many symptoms of anxiety. They can be broadly categorised as either physical or psychological.

Physical

- Palpitations
- Sweating
- Tremor
- Dry mouth
- Difficulty breathing
- Choking
- Chest tightness
- Abdominal pain/ discomfort/nausea
- Hot flushes
- Tingling in fingers

Psychological

- Dizziness
- Fear of losing control
- Fear of dying
- Feeling out of it
- Loss of appetite
- Poor sleep
- Tiredness
- Feeling on edge
- Restlessness
- Difficulty concentrating
- Depression

- We sweat; this happens in order to cool us down but at the same time we may feel cold because adrenaline has caused the blood to drain away from the skin.

- We feel on edge and tense because all our senses and muscles have been pepped up.

None of these symptoms will cause a problem to us. The body has it all under control. We do not even notice them when we experience them in the appropriate situation – a threatening situation. We do notice them, however, if we experience them when we are not being threatened. We also notice them if the threat goes on for a long time or if our response is out of proportion to the threat that we perceive.

How anxiety makes you feel

Symptoms of anxiety are caused by our fight, fright or flight response. The easiest way to remember them is if they are grouped under four headings:

1. Symptoms resulting from the nervous system being pepped up
2. Symptoms involving the chest and stomach
3. Psychological symptoms
4. Secondary symptoms.

Nervous system

There are four major symptoms that people experience because the nervous system is hyperactive when we are anxious:

1. Palpitations: the feeling that your heart is beating too fast.
2. Sweating: this is the result of the effect of adrenaline on the sweat glands.
3. Trembling: this is because adrenaline has fired up your sensory system and muscles ready for action. It is as if you are on the grid at the front of a Formula One racetrack ready to start.
4. Dry mouth: this is because of the effect of adrenaline on the salivary glands – you do not need to be eating at a time like this!

The chest and stomach

There are four major symptoms:

1. Some people feel that they are finding it difficult to breathe. This is usually because the nervous system is sending messages telling you to breathe more quickly. This is so that more oxygen shoots into the bloodstream.

2. Some people feel like they are choking. This is a complex feeling that is to do with the effect of adrenaline on digestion and a little to do with the effects of fear hormones on breathing.

3. Chest pain: tightness in the chest is often felt because the heart is pounding and breathing has quickened.

4. Nausea or abdominal pain and churning: this is because the body has directed blood away from the stomach. It is also because of an effect of hormones on the muscles of the digestive tract. They can be broadly categorised as either physical or psychological. Everything is put on hold.

Psychological symptoms

1. Dizziness, unsteadiness, light-headed feelings and feeling faint. These all occur because of changes in blood pressure, the amount of oxygen in the blood and the direction of blood flow during anxiety.

2. Fear of losing control: some people misunderstand all the changes that are happening to their body and fear that they are losing control or going crazy. This is a misinterpretation of a complex and very controlled physiological response.

3. Fear of dying: not surprisingly, if someone is feeling

chest pain, having difficulty in breathing and feeling faint, some people think that they are having a heart attack or some other serious condition. A classic symptom of some forms of anxiety is the fear that all these bodily symptoms mean that you are physically ill.

4. Feeling out of it: some people feel like they are detached from their body and that everything is happening to someone else. This is a common symptom of anxiety. It works at a subconscious level and is not under voluntary control. It's a trick that is played by the mind. If a person does not think that the threatening situation is actually happening to him or her, you can see how this may help a person feel calmer. However, having this feeling over a longer period of time is very unpleasant. (Think what it would be like if your child came home happy and pleased to see you and you just felt cold and detached.)

Secondary symptoms

1. Hot flushes and cold chills: these occur because of the effects of adrenaline on the blood supply to the skin and the sweat glands. Cold chills are caused by the initial constriction of the blood vessels, but when they are allowed to relax a lot of blood flows in – hence the hot flushes.

2. Numbness or tingling: the nervous system is pepped up by adrenaline and this sometimes shows itself as numbness or tingling in the fingers. The tension that is felt in the muscles can also lead to tingling and numbness.

Changes in social behaviour

In addition to physical symptoms of the fight, fright or flight reaction, long-term anxiety can change our lives. If fears and anxieties go on for some time we run into further problems. We change our behaviour to deal with them. We can become tired, depressed, slowed down and restless, and we may lose our appetite. Sleeping can become difficult and we may have bad dreams. We also try to avoid further frightening experiences and may withdraw from life.

The symptoms of a panic attack

Some people feel anxious all the time but other people experience an intense, but relatively brief, fear reaction. This is called a panic attack.

It starts abruptly, reaches a maximum within a few minutes and lasts from a few minutes to half an hour. For it to be classed as a panic attack, there must be a feeling of intense fear and at least four of the physical symptoms of anxiety in the box on page 15.

People who have panic attacks often try to avoid the situation in which they experience the panic. Some people who are inside at the time find that opening a window helps.

The bodily changes in a panic attack are exactly the same as the bodily changes in fear and anxiety. That is why the symptoms are so similar. The thing about panic attacks is that they occur intensely, there is usually no threat and, even if there is a threat, most people would agree that the threat is not severe enough to lead to panic. Panic attacks come out of nowhere. Although they are frightening, the bodily changes are not anything that will cause problems.

Panic attacks have a way of making sure that they perpetuate themselves. During a panic attack it is easy to think that the symptoms that you have mean that you are very ill. Many people with panic attacks fix on one thought – 'does this mean I am ill?' – and fixing on that thought makes them more anxious and makes the attack still fiercer.

Hyperventilation syndrome

During an attack of anxiety some people breathe quickly and their breathing is very shallow. Quick shallow breathing (hyperventilation) causes more carbon dioxide to be exhaled, which decreases the acid content of the blood. This results in tingling of the fingers and light-headedness, and can cause muscles to cramp. There is a feeling of tightness in the chest. Not surprisingly all these symptoms lead to a vicious circle – during an attack you become more anxious and think that you have a serious physical illness. The truth is that none of these symptoms will cause any lasting problem. As soon as you start breathing properly they go away. Their main significance is that some doctors misdiagnose the blood changes as other conditions and give people the wrong treatment.

Hyperventilation can occur in many anxiety disorders and can occur out of nowhere during unaccustomed exercise, such as scuba diving. Some people think that anxiety disorder is a diagnosis in itself.

One way of dealing with hyperventilation is to re-breathe into a paper bag. The air in the bag will undergo a slow increase in carbon dioxide levels as you re-breathe. As a result of this, the level of carbon dioxide in your blood will get back to normal. However, some people find this difficult to do; instead they find it easier to be taught to slow their breathing down, taking deeper breaths. Keeping the length of inspiration and expiration the same is important.

KEY POINTS

- We respond to fear by pepping up our nervous system and releasing hormones into our bloodstream

- The same things are going on in the body during both fear and anxiety

- The symptoms of anxiety and fear are all the result of our natural defence mechanisms against attack

- There are four groups of anxiety symptoms: nervous system symptoms, chest and stomach symptoms, psychological symptoms and secondary symptoms

Theories of anxiety

There are three issues covered in this next section: first, who is at risk of anxiety, second, what the underlying changes in the body are that cause the symptoms of anxiety and, third, how anxiety develops into an anxiety disorder.

Who is at risk?

In general women are at greater risk than men. Nobody knows why this is.

Genetic, psychological and social factors are all important in an individual's risk of developing an anxiety problem. However, because there are so many factors involved (some that make anxiety more likely, others that make anxiety less likely) it is difficult to predict who will develop a problem.

The rates of anxiety problems are different throughout the world. It would seem that some cultures produce less anxiety than others. Research has shown high rates of anxiety disorders in New Zealand and low rates in some east Asian countries. Within a country the rates of anxiety problems are different for different groups. For instance, in the USA African–Americans have high rates of anxiety disorders. No one knows why rates are higher in certain areas and among certain groups than others, but differences in the way different groups see the world, support each other and set up their societies are considered important.

It is easy to imagine that anxiety may be more likely if you live in an inner city area with a high crime rate and where lots of different people come and go than if you live in a village where you were brought up and know most of the people. In the UK you are 50 per cent more likely to have an anxiety problem if you live in a city compared with if you live in the countryside.

Genetic factors

There are a number of lines of evidence that indicate that your genes are important in the development of anxiety. For instance, close relatives of patients who have a specific phobia are more likely to have a specific phobia themselves than people who do not have a family member with a specific phobia. The same is true of panic disorder.

Social factors

Anxiety disorders are more common at the time of important life events such as examinations, death of a spouse or, in the case of post-traumatic stress disorder, after life-threatening incidents. Proper support at such times decreases the risk of developing anxiety. Proper preparation for predictable events such as exams, leaving home to go to college or starting a new job can decrease the chance of these events causing anxiety problems.

What is happening in the body?
The biochemistry

As we have discussed, in response to fear, certain chemicals (hormones) are released in the body. Most of the symptoms of the fear response are caused by the effects of these hormones – adrenaline (epinephrine) and noradrenaline (norepinephrine, a cousin of adrenaline) – on the body.

In anxiety – long-term fear – certain brain chemicals are also affected. These include serotonin and gamma-aminobutyric acid (GABA). Serotonin is well known because it is important in depression and GABA is important in relaxation.

There are many other brain chemicals that have been implicated but our knowledge of these is currently not extensive.

If you have an anxiety problem the balance of the brain chemicals that are important in the fear response may be disturbed. Too much of a response is produced. It is not clear what causes brain chemicals to reach different levels and act differently in people with anxiety problems. Some scientists believe that differences in response to fear may be a genetic vulnerability that is triggered by a traumatic event. Others believe that the changes in brain chemicals that scientists see are a result of anxiety rather than a cause.

Adrenaline

Direct action of this hormone on nerve cells leads to many of the symptoms of anxiety. It has effects on the blood cells, the skin, the gut, the brain, the heart and the lungs.

Noradrenaline

Scientists believe that increased action of this chemical is important in the development of anxiety and panic attacks.

Laboratory studies have demonstrated that activation of nerves containing noradrenaline can cause anxiety. They have also shown that high levels of the by-products of noradrenaline are found in the brain system when people are anxious.

Serotonin

There are many different actions of serotonin in the brain. Serotonin seems to be important in depression. It is a chemical that acts as a messenger between nerve cells and may not be working effectively in people who are depressed. Increased serotonin activity can lead to anxiety. However, increased serotonin over a period of time also seems to calm people down, perhaps because it also has an effect on changing the concentrations of other chemicals in the brain. Many of the drugs used in the treatment of anxiety disorders have an effect on serotonin.

GABA

Nerves containing GABA in the brain generally calm people down. Scientists believe that in anxiety GABA activity is decreased. Some drugs prescribed for anxiety are thought to work by pepping up the function of the GABA-containing nerves.

How does anxiety develop into an anxiety disorder?
Psychoanalytical theories

Psychoanalysts, the best known of whom was Sigmund

Freud, believe that the mind consists of different components: the conscious part and the subconscious. The conscious part of the mind deals with fears and desires. If these fears and desires are sometimes difficult to deal with, rather than resolving those that it cannot cope with, the mind will try to forget or bury them in the subconscious. Unfortunately, this may not work and when the fear or desire tries to express itself it presents as anxiety. Sigmund Freud, working in Austria at the start of the twentieth century, believed that anxiety disorders in some of the women whom he treated were the result of sexual desires that they could not cope with or discuss because they were considered unbecoming of a lady.

Learning theory
The theory is that anxiety is a fear that has been attached to the wrong stimulus. We learn to be scared of the wrong thing or react in an inappropriate way to certain situations and this soon becomes habit. The more we do it the more it becomes habit. For instance, panic attacks and fears produce a vicious circle that keeps them going.

The panic comes out of nowhere. People think that they are developing a heart condition. As a result of this they monitor their heart. Thinking about your heart can make it beat faster. You realise that your heart is beating quickly and so convince yourself that you have a heart problem. So your anxiety grows.

Fears can spiral out of control in the same way. One of the things people like least about spiders is the fact that they are unpredictable. Many people who have spider phobias (arachnophobia) will not go near them and will not look at them. Not going near them and not looking at them make them all the more mysterious and, so, all the more unpredictable and all the more frightening. As a result of this, not going near them or looking at them makes them even more anxiety provoking.

Running away or avoiding the spider (or another fear) increases the fear in another way. If you are anxious and you run away from the situation you teach

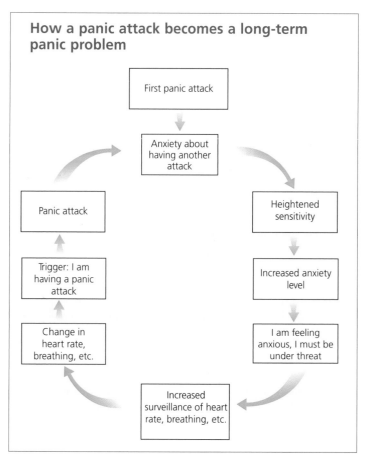

How a panic attack becomes a long-term panic problem

First panic attack

Anxiety about having another attack

Heightened sensitivity

Increased anxiety level

I am feeling anxious, I must be under threat

Increased surveillance of heart rate, breathing, etc.

Change in heart rate, breathing, etc.

Trigger: I am having a panic attack

Panic attack

yourself two lessons: the spider causes the anxiety and the only way you can control it is by running away. You teach yourself that being afraid of spiders is part of how you are. The truth is that we make ourselves frightened and we can control it. We can control it without running away. Running away makes our fears grow and stops us taking control.

Childhood and modelling

If we stay with the fear of spiders, as an example, some children develop a fear of them because they see family members becoming anxious or scared when they are around. Children may lodge in their brains that spiders are animals to be scared of and this fear will surface when they see a spider. If they run away from the spider or lift up their feet so that it cannot touch them, the symptoms of fear will go away. They will have taught themselves two lessons: spiders cause fear and avoiding them relieves the fear.

Learning to be afraid of something because of an accident

Other people learn to be afraid because of chance happenings or accidents – falling off a bike or having an accident is liable to make you anxious the next time that you are asked to use one. If you put off getting back on the bike it becomes more and more scary. You become anxious if you think about riding a bike and, if you decide not to do it, that anxiety goes. Again, you teach yourself that bikes are anxiety provoking and not using them makes you less anxious. The longer you leave it, the more anxiety provoking it becomes – that is why people say once you have fallen off a bike the best thing is to get back on straight away. Facing your fears stops them growing.

In agoraphobia some people tell of having a panic attack when in a crowded place and running home for sanctuary. They link being outside with having a panic attack and because they do not want to have one they stay indoors. They have taught themselves that staying in makes them symptom free and going out produces a panic attack.

We perpetuate our own fears by not facing them. Other people sometimes help us do the same. For instance, a person with agoraphobia may ask his partner to accompany him when he goes out – in case something happens. Many agree because they do not want partners to suffer and when they go out the partners say, 'I feel better when you are here'. This can make the problem worse. People with agoraphobia still think that going out causes panic plus they have now taught themselves that they need to rely on their partner. They have 'learned' that they need help in order to go out.

KEY POINTS

- The symptoms of anxiety are caused by well-understood physical reactions

- The reasons why some people do and others do not develop anxiety disorders are complex

- Our genes, brain chemicals, hormones and social circumstances are all important causes of anxiety problems

- We can teach ourselves to be anxious by the way we respond to threatening events

- We can perpetuate anxiety by not facing up to our fears – we learn that it is easier to avoid the situation

Types of anxiety problems

What type of anxiety problem?

If your anxiety or fear is severe, persistent and out of proportion to the threat, and causes problems with your everyday life, you are suffering from an anxiety disorder.

Anxiety problems all present themselves with some of the anxiety symptoms that we have described earlier. They can be classified into four groups:

1. Anxiety resulting from physical illness

2. Phobic anxiety problems: the situation, event or relationship that is causing the anxiety can be easily identified

3. Non-phobic anxiety problems: the situation, event or relationship that currently causes the anxiety disorder cannot be recognised

4. Other anxiety problems, such as obsessive–compulsive disorder and post-traumatic stress disorder, that do not fit into any of the above categories.

What distinguishes one type of anxiety problem from another is what causes the symptoms and the pattern of the symptoms. For instance, the difference between two anxiety problems such as a phobia and a generalised anxiety disorder is the cause of the symptoms. The fear response in a phobia is produced by a specific situation such as coming into contact with birds – as an example – but people with generalised anxiety disorder often cannot pinpoint a particular situation that causes their anxiety symptoms.

The difference between generalised anxiety syndrome and another anxiety problem, for instance panic disorder, is the pattern of the symptoms of anxiety. In generalised anxiety, symptoms are there all the time, whereas people with panic attacks experience intense anxiety that lasts a short period of time but can feel all right between attacks.

There are no laboratory tests that help to diagnose anxiety disorders. Doctors may perform tests but these are to make sure that the anxiety symptoms are not caused by a physical illness (see pages 33–5). As a result of this, whether or not you have one anxiety disorder or another depends on you, your doctor, therapist or friend sitting down and working through when you experience your symptoms and what your symptoms are like.

Once this has been done your symptoms can be compared with the sets of symptoms and causes of the symptoms for different medical categories of anxiety. As we are all different, the mixture of symptoms that each individual has may vary and it may be that you do not fit neatly into a particular category.

Why is it useful to categorise anxiety problems?

Some people claim that these categories and labels are not important – labels are for objects, not for people. This may be true but if you can group people with specific types of problems together you can set up specific types of therapy. There are different ways of helping a person who has a fear of spiders, for example, and a person who has a generalised anxiety but cannot identify the source. Some forms of treatment work for one type of anxiety disorder, but not another, so it is important to identify the type of anxiety that you have.

It cannot be stressed too strongly that you may not have all the symptoms that are seen in a particular condition. You may have a mixture of symptoms from different conditions and you may have more than one condition at a time. In addition, because serious anxiety problems are so distressing, some people with anxiety problems also develop depression.

The important thing to note is that these diagnoses are guidelines rather than something set in stone. If you do not fit into a particular category it simply reflects the fact that people are unique and human suffering is difficult to fit into neat boxes. It does not mean that you are more ill than other people or that you have a problem that no one can treat. The feature that is common to all these problems is anxiety and the symptoms of anxiety are caused by a well-understood and predictable physical reaction that can be treated.

Anxiety resulting from physical illness

There are many medical conditions that cause anxiety symptoms. If you see a doctor about your anxiety he or she will ask you in detail about your symptoms and when they began, how long they last at any one time, what causes them and what helps them go away.

You will also be asked about your general physical health and whether or not you are taking any prescribed medication and if you take any drugs or remedies that have not been prescribed, including recreational and over-the-counter drugs. The doctor may enquire about your mental health. Depression is one of the most common reasons for anxiety.

Most people who go to a doctor with anxiety do not have any physical problem but doctors are trained to be thorough and systematic and so they will try to satisfy themselves that you are otherwise in good health. Don't be worried by this, it is routine practice.

Medical conditions that can cause anxiety symptoms

A number of drugs can cause anxiety. Perhaps the best-known drug is the caffeine found in tea and coffee, and others include the nicotine in tobacco. Prescribed drugs, for instance some asthma medications, can cause anxiety, as can steroids, for example those taken orally for an inflammatory condition.

Taking too much of a prescribed drug can lead to anxiety symptoms so it is important that your doctor knows what you are taking and that you are aware of potential side effects.

Recreational drugs such as amphetamines and cocaine can cause anxiety. Many drugs, both prescribed and non-prescribed, can cause anxiety when you stop taking them. Regular alcohol drinkers experience withdrawal symptoms, which include anxiety, when they stop drinking. People who stop taking sleeping pills often become anxious. Some of the older drugs used to treat anxiety can lead to worsening anxiety when they are stopped. People who use heroin develop anxiety as part of their withdrawal.

A variety of medical conditions can cause anxiety. Going to the doctor or worrying about being ill is anxiety provoking in itself, but some medical conditions produce anxiety symptoms as part of the illness. An example is hyperthyroidism. In hyperthyroidism the high levels of thyroid hormones circulating in the blood produce symptoms that can be indistinguishable from generalised anxiety disorder.

The most common hormonal cause of anxiety symptoms is probably premenstrual syndrome resulting from changes in female sex hormones. Anxiety symptoms are also common during the menopause (the time around when a woman's periods stop). A number of other endocrine (hormone) problems are characterised by prominent symptoms of anxiety.

Heart and lung problems can produce anxiety, both because of their effects on our bodies and because we worry about them. It is difficult not to worry when you feel short of breath.

A diverse range of other medical conditions, from stomach ulcers through to epilepsy and copper poisoning, can produce anxiety symptoms.

Other mental health problems can cause anxiety. Most people with depression also have anxiety symptoms and some who have hallucinations or delusions have anxiety.

Phobic anxiety problems

In phobic anxiety there is fear or anxiety in response to a particular object or event. In phobic anxiety the thing or event has to be real and in the outside world

– not just in your imagination. It is not simply a worry about events that happened in the past. The most common forms of this are agoraphobia, social phobia and simple phobias.

We can all recognise that there are objects or situations that we do not like or for which we claim we are phobic. This is not what doctors are concerned about. A phobia impairs your day-to-day activity or stops you doing something that you want to do, so it needs to be treated. Many people dislike flying. They find it scary but they cope with it. However, one flying phobic I treated missed her son's wedding because she could not board a plane. She would have loved to have gone, but could not. She had avoided flying because of her phobia and had realised how serious her phobia was only when there was too little time to treat it before the wedding.

In phobic anxiety, the anxiety and fear symptoms are present, or predominantly present, only in certain well-defined situations that are not currently dangerous. The fear or anxiety needs to be so intense that these situations are avoided or endured only with dread because there is no alternative. As a result of the severity of the response, the individual starts to worry about physical symptoms or becomes concerned that he or she is going mad or losing control. All of this leads to anxiety in anticipation of coming into contact with the feared object or event.

Many people with phobic anxiety disorders also suffer depression. Some people become so phobic that they develop panic attacks either when they come into contact with the feared thing or, in very severe cases, even when they think about the subject of their phobia.

People with severe phobic anxiety states restrict their daily activities because of their anxiety or fear. This may lead to negative life consequences. For instance, a person who develops agoraphobia may be unable to leave the house. This may lead to unemployment. It is not always completely clear what the problem is. I have sometimes been sent patients from chest physicians because they have not been able to treat their breathing problems, such as shortness of breath. It is only after detailed questioning that it has become obvious that they have difficulty in breathing only in certain situations and that they are scared of that situation.

Agoraphobia
What is it?

Agoraphobia means fear of the market place (from the Greek word *agora* meaning market place). This is one of the most common types of phobia. In agoraphobia there are a number of fears. They are all to do with leaving the home or other safe places and entering other places (shops, crowds or public places) where the person feels vulnerable or trapped.

Many people with agoraphobia develop panic attacks and deal with anxiety by not going out. This of course makes going out even more fearsome. Others feel they can go out only if accompanied by a friend, in case something goes wrong; this quickly leads to dependence on that friend and does not help resolve the agoraphobia.

The symptoms vary considerably from person to person and throughout the course of the illness. Some people describe their agoraphobia slowly worsening and restricting them, so that they do less and less over a period of time.

Case history – agoraphobia

A typical story is of a woman who has a panic attack while coming home from the shops. She gets home as soon as possible and, of course, by the time she is home the panic attack has stopped.

After this she becomes more worried when in crowds and looks for signs that the intense symptoms of panic will come back. She cannot relax at all when she goes out and becomes increasingly anxious. She gets so anxious that she starts to develop the very same symptoms of anxiety that she feared would return. Once the symptoms appear she goes home to try to escape them.

Her mind learns two lessons from this: first, that she was right to be concerned about going out – it does cause symptoms – second, that she was right that she should stay at home – going home gets rid of the symptoms. So the vicious circle starts.

Agoraphobia is sometimes difficult to understand and recognise because, if someone who has it is seen at home, in her safe place, or with the person who supports her, she may not seem that anxious. This is because she is completely avoiding the situation that makes her anxious – being away from her anxiety-provoking place and alone.

How common is it?
Rates of agoraphobia vary around the world. In some places in the east 1 in 100 people suffers anxiety; on some Caribbean islands the rate is seven times higher. Nobody knows why. In most places women are twice as likely to develop it as men. There is some evidence that the rates are higher in cities than in the countryside.

The onset of agoraphobia is typically between 18 and 35 years of age.

When people look back at what started their agoraphobia they often find that it happened at a time when they were feeling very stressed. It is as if they are all tensed up and tipped into a panic attack by something else. This more often than not happens in a public place – we all become anxious in these situations.

How is it diagnosed?

For doctors to diagnose agoraphobia the following must all be present:

- There is fear or avoidance of at least two of the following: crowds, public places, travelling alone or travelling away from home.
- There are at least two of the symptoms of anxiety (see page 15).
- The problem causes significant emotional distress by either the symptoms it causes or the necessity of having to avoid certain situations.
- The symptoms are present only when in the feared situation or when thinking about the feared situation.
- The symptoms are not a result of other psychiatric problems such as hallucinations, delusions or depression.
- Physical causes of anxiety have been ruled out and the anxiety is not the result of cultural beliefs.

In general, if you regularly avoid situations because you are frightened of having panic attacks or if you avoid being outside your home, standing in queues, or being at home alone, in crowded places or in open places such as a park because they make you feel anxious, you should consider visiting your GP for an assessment. If you find it too difficult to visit your GP, ask your GP to visit you.

Social phobia
What is it?
Social phobia is an exaggeration of something that many of us experience. In social phobia there is fear of being the centre of attention. This leads to avoidance of social situations. The symptoms may be blushing, shaking, sweating, a desperate need to go to the toilet or panic attacks. There is also a fear that other people may notice your anxious behaviour – they may see you blushing, for instance. The fear is that you will behave in an embarrassing way.

Some people have a specific social phobia where one situation makes them anxious, such as eating in public, but many people have a number of situations that they fear.

Lots of people become anxious when they are scrutinised by others. For it to be classed as social phobia, however, you would have to avoid the situation. In severe social phobia sufferers withdraw from all social contact.

How common is it?
Across the world the rates of social phobia vary. In Taiwan 2 in 1,000 people have social phobia whereas in New Zealand the rate is 20 times higher. Within any country the people with less money and less education tend to suffer more from social phobia. Most people develop it in late puberty or early adult life.

Social withdrawal and low self-esteem are risk factors for depression, so not surprisingly people with social phobia are more likely to be depressed. One method of dealing with social anxiety is to drink alcohol when you are in public. So, again, not surprisingly people with social phobia are more likely to develop alcohol problems.

How is it diagnosed?

The following are the criteria that doctors use to diagnose social phobia:

- You fear being the centre of attention, fear behaving in a way that is humiliating or avoid being the centre of attention or in situations in which there is a possibility of behaving in an embarrassing way.

- Fear in social situations such as eating or speaking in public, encountering known individuals in public or entering or enduring small group situations.

- At least two of the symptoms of anxiety are present (see page 15) in these situations and at least one of the following symptoms: blushing or shaking; fear of vomiting; fear of passing urine or opening your bowels.

- Significant emotional distress is caused by the problem and the person who suffers from it realises that his worries are excessive.

- The symptoms are restricted to certain situations and are not the result of other mental health problems or physical disorders.

A general rule is that, if you worry a lot about behaving in an embarrassing way, what people might think of you or being anxious in a social situation, or you avoid public speaking, eating out or parties, you may have social phobia and should consider seeing your GP for advice.

Simple phobias
What is it?
A phobia is an irrational fear of an object or situation. For it to be classed as a phobia either the situation or object would not bother most people or your reaction is excessive compared with that of others.

These are phobias restricted to highly specific situations such as being close to particular objects, for example certain animals, heights, thunder, lightning or flying. Going into the situation produces symptoms of anxiety and panic just as it would in social phobia or agoraphobia. In general, the heart rate goes up and the blood pressure rises as a result of the adrenaline rush. However, in one type of phobia – needle phobia – the opposite happens. People have a sudden drop in blood pressure and feel faint.

Not surprisingly people avoid the situation or whatever it is that makes them scared.

In contrast to other anxiety problems, these sorts of phobias usually develop in childhood or adolescence. Animal phobias and blood phobias usually develop before the age of 10 and dental phobias have an average age of onset of 12 years. However, claustrophobia has an average age of onset of 20.

How is it diagnosed?
Simple phobias vary considerably in severity. To be diagnosed as having a specific phobia you must have the following:

- You have a marked fear of a specific object or

situation that is not one of those listed under agoraphobia.

- You avoid that situation because of fear and feel symptoms of anxiety.
- The fear is restricted to the feared situation and causes significant emotional distress.

People with specific phobias usually recognise that their fears are unreasonably excessive.

There is a long list of objects and situations that people have become phobic for, but the most common are animals, birds, insects, heights, thunder, flying, small enclosed spaces, the sight of blood or injury, injections, dentists and hospitals.

Non-phobic anxiety problems

Sometimes anxiety seems to come out of nowhere. Exactly what triggers the anxiety is not easy to pinpoint. There are a number of conditions, known as non-phobic anxiety problems, where anxiety is a major symptom but it is not restricted to a particular situation or triggered by a particular event or object. Many people who have these problems also show symptoms of depression and they may also have phobic problems. Doctors make a diagnosis of a non-phobic anxiety problem if the most severe symptoms are those of anxiety symptoms with an unknown cause.

Examples of these problems are panic disorder, generalised anxiety, and mixed anxiety and depression.

Panic disorder
What is it?
Some people have recurrent attacks of severe anxiety. These are not restricted to any particular situation.

Often the symptoms include a sudden onset of palpitations, chest pain, choking sensations, dizziness and a feeling of unreality. As a result of the suddenness of the symptoms, some people fear that they are dying, they will lose control or they are going mad. There is an overwhelming feeling of doom. These fears make the panic more intense. Most panic attacks occur for no reason but some are brought on by strong emotion or excitement.

Many people suffer in silence with their panic problems. The frequency of attacks varies and sometimes they completely disappear. The number and intensity of attacks sometimes depend on the amount of stress in a person's life. There are more panic attacks at stressful times and fewer when life is easier. However, for most people the number of panic attacks bears no relationship at all to other events that are happening in their lives.

Life events such as the death of a spouse may be linked to the development of depression and some other anxiety problems but do not seem to be linked to the development of panic.

Panic can be so distressing that it leads to depression in about half of the people who have it. Others may try to treat panic themselves with alcohol. This makes the situation worse rather than better. One in five people with panic disorder has alcohol abuse problems.

Many people with agoraphobia have panic attacks. Indeed, it is sometimes a panic attack that leads to agoraphobia.

Although they are very frightening and the symptoms are intense, panic attacks often last only a few minutes and they go of their own accord. However, the symptoms are so distressing and debilitating that if they occur regularly they need treatment.

How are they diagnosed?

Panic attacks are pretty easy to diagnose. The important task for a doctor is to make sure that they are not caused by something else. They will try to make sure that they are not the result of a particular event or situation. If so, it would be classed as a phobia. They will make sure that they are not the result of being in a dangerous or life-threatening situation, when they would be classed as post-traumatic problems.

The attack itself is characterised by intense fear and discomfort and has an easily definable start and finish. It will start abruptly, reach a maximum intensity within a few minutes and last for some minutes.

During the attack symptoms include at least one of:

- palpitations or pounding heart, or fast heart rate
- sweating
- trembling or shaking
- dry mouth

and at least three more symptoms of anxiety (see page 15).

These symptoms and the panic are not the result of other mental health problems or a physical condition.

Sometimes doctors grade panic attacks as moderate or severe, depending on how often the attacks occur:

- Moderate panic attacks – defined as at least four attacks in a four-week period.
- Severe panic attacks – at least four panic attacks a week for four weeks.

Panic problems usually develop in the late teens or early twenties. Women are up to three times more likely to suffer from panic attacks than men.

In general, panic disorder is diagnosed if you have experienced sudden attacks of intense anxiety or fear during which you felt that you were going to die, lose control or go crazy. If you worry about having more of these attacks, if you have tried to change what you do because you think you know what triggers these attacks and if you worry about the physical symptoms you have during the attacks, you should visit your doctor for an assessment.

Generalised anxiety disorder
What is it?
This is another anxiety problem in which it is difficult to find a specific trigger for the symptoms. Undue apprehension or worry rules the life of a person who has this. As we all worry from time to time, the symptoms would need to exist for at least six months before they would be considered to be a problem. All or any of the symptoms of anxiety can be present. The presence of the physical symptoms of anxiety cause concern, which leads to increased anxiety.

It is called generalised anxiety because it is not caused by any particular object or situation and it is there all the time – unlike panic, which starts abruptly, lasts for a few minutes and then goes away.

Women are about twice as likely to develop generalised anxiety. It can start at any age but the average age of onset is 21. Many people with generalised anxiety say that they have been anxious all their lives, but stressful events in their lives make their anxiety worse. Others say that they have never been anxious but a particularly stressful time in their life has made them anxious and the anxiety has not gone away.

Many people suffer anxiety for years but the symptoms come and go over time. If left untreated it can lead to other problems. Many people with generalised anxiety also have mild, moderate or severe depression or panic disorder.

How is it diagnosed?

As anxiety may coexist with other problems diagnosis can sometimes be difficult. For a diagnosis of generalised anxiety disorder to be made, anxiety would need to be persistent, and not restricted to or even predominantly suffered in any particular circumstance or situation. Symptoms are those of anxiety. At least four symptoms would be present and there would be prominent tension, worry and feelings of apprehension about everyday events and problems. In addition, sufferers may worry that a close friend or relative, or indeed themselves, may become ill.

The symptoms are not caused by a physical illness, mental illness or drug withdrawal.

Generally, if you have been feeling nervous or on edge most of the time over the past six months, if you have problems falling asleep, if you feel muscular tension because of feeling on edge and if you frequently feel tense and irritable, you may have generalised anxiety disorder and should consider seeing your GP.

Mixed anxiety and depression

In some people symptoms of anxiety and depression are present in equal measure but neither is strong enough to warrant a diagnosis of depression or anxiety.

Other anxiety disorders
Obsessive–compulsive disorder
What is it?

In obsessive–compulsive disorder (OCD) anxiety is produced by a *thought* rather than a situation, event or object.

Obsessional thoughts are ideas, images or impulses that enter a person's mind again and again. They are distressing and cause anxiety. Although the thoughts occur involuntarily, you know that they are your thoughts and come from your subconscious, but you are unable to control them.

Attempts to resist the thoughts do not work and so something has to be done about them, for instance if you are worried about contamination then you need to wash your hands.

Typical thoughts include fear of contamination, doubt that the doors and windows are locked so that burglars can break in, or worries that something you do or forget to do may cause harm to yourself or others. Obsessional thoughts can take an almost infinite variety of forms – as varied as people themselves are.

One of my patient's obsessive thoughts was that he would abuse children even though he found the idea repugnant and had brought up his children with no problems whatsoever. He was no danger at all to children but he could not be convinced of this.

Another of my patients never threw a piece of paper away during her entire life. She feared that she would lose important information that she would never be able to find again. Her house was completely full of paper; every room from floor to ceiling was stacked with paper by the time she was 45.

One way of decreasing the anxiety caused by obsessive thoughts is by doing something to reassure yourself that there is not a problem. If you are worried about being contaminated you may wash you hands. If you are concerned that you may not have locked the doors and windows properly you may check them. The steps that you take to decrease the anxiety caused by obsessive thoughts are called compulsions.

The problem is that compulsions often do not banish the anxiety or the obsessive thought and so they have to be repeated over and over again. You may lock all the doors and windows in your house but by the time you have returned upstairs and into bed the obsessive thought comes back – did you lock all the doors and windows properly? You try to resist it and go to sleep but it comes back again and because of this you go downstairs and do it all again.

In general, performing the compulsion makes the obsession worse. Instead of simply ignoring the thought, you are acting upon it – giving credence to the obsession.

Some people try to resolve this by having a routine and method to performing the compulsion, be it locking doors and windows or washing their hands. If they keep to their routine they believe that it will be easier to resist the obsessive thoughts and decrease their anxieties. For instance, they can say to themselves 'I have washed my hands three times using soap and water and used a clean towel. I cannot be contaminated'. However, far from decreasing the anxiety, compulsive acts can increase it. More questions arise, not only 'Are my hands dirty?', but now 'Did I do my handwashing routine properly? Should I do it again?'.

Compulsive acts are not tasks that are enjoyable. Most people who do them recognise that they are not useful. They are performed simply to reduce anxiety of an unlikely event that a person fears may happen because of their obsessive thoughts.

Once obsessive thoughts and compulsive acts become linked, attempts to resist either of them lead to anxiety.

The severity of obsessive–compulsive problems is very variable. Many people have some obsessive thoughts and checking and washing are very common. However, in OCD the problem is of another magnitude. Hours of each day may be spent checking and washing. Once ready to leave the house, it may take a very long time, sometimes hours, to leave the house because everything has to be checked and checked again. Similarly, getting to sleep at night is delayed by a ritual of closing, checking and rechecking every door and window. Despite the repeated checking, there is often significant anxiety.

The most common anxiety is that of contamination. Some studies show that 50 per cent of people with OCD have this problem. It is usually focused on contamination with urine or faeces. A typical person with a fear of contamination will spend hours each day washing his or her hands or bathing. He or she may also try to avoid possible sources of contamination – but this is not usually successful.

Not everyone with OCD has obsessions and compulsions. Some people simply have obsessive thoughts that go round and round in their heads, winding them up and provoking anxiety, and some people lose their obsessive ideas and simply have compulsions.

How common is it?
Both men and women can develop OCD. The problem is common. Between one and three per cent of the

population have OCD, but the figure may be higher than this because most people with this problem suffer in silence. They often receive treatment only long after the problem has started. This is unfortunate because the earlier the OCD is treated the more likely is treatment to be successful.

Obsessive–compulsive problems usually start in adolescence but they can occur at any age. Some people say that the problems first started after a stressful event but many people cannot pinpoint what triggered the problem.

There are also physical causes of the condition. Some people who have had severe head injuries or brain infections develop obsessive–compulsive problems, but these causes are very rare.

How is it diagnosed?

For doctors to make a diagnosis of OCD a person will have suffered from obsessions or compulsions every day for at least two weeks. The obsessions or compulsions will have caused distress or interfered with social or individual functioning, usually by wasting time. The obsession or compulsion is not the consequence of any other mental illness.

Post-traumatic stress disorder
What is it?

This is a delayed and/or protracted response to a stressful event or situation. The situation that has caused the response is exceptionally threatening or catastrophic in nature. It is the type of problem that is likely to cause distress in most people.

Most stress problems after a traumatic event settle down of their own accord. Doctors tend to treat problems only if they have been present for some months or more.

Some people are more prone to developing post-traumatic stress problems than others. People who are a bit obsessive, who depend a lot on others and who are anxious seem to be more likely to show post-traumatic reactions. However, most people who develop post-traumatic stress do not have those sorts of personalities.

The symptoms of post-traumatic stress disorder vary from person to person. Typical features include episodes of repeated reliving of the trauma by flashbacks, dreams or nightmares. Many people feel persistent numbness and detachment from other people. Many avoid situations that remind them of the trauma and exhibit a general unresponsiveness to their surroundings, not being able to derive joy from activities that used to give pleasure. Most people with post-traumatic stress disorder feel on edge most of the time. They are hyper-alert, become easily startled and find it difficult to sleep.

Perhaps surprisingly, many people find it difficult to recall, either partly or completely, some important aspects of the stressful event that caused the post-traumatic problem. Not surprisingly, depression is common, as it is in many of the anxiety problems. Some people are so distressed by their situation that they consider suicide as a solution.

Post-traumatic stress disorder can be traced back to a particular event. However, the problem usually does not develop for weeks and sometimes even months after. Once it has developed symptoms vary in their intensity but most people will recover. However, a minority of cases take years to recover and the sufferer develops some change in personality.

How is it diagnosed?

Doctors usually make the diagnosis of post-traumatic stress disorder if:

- you have been exposed to a severe traumatic event
- you have persistent remembering or reliving of the event such as dreams or flashbacks, or you become nervous when experiencing circumstances resembling those of the stressful situation
- you avoid such situations
- you cannot recall important parts of what happened
- you show symptoms of psychological sensitivity such as difficulty falling asleep or staying asleep, irritability and outbursts of anger or difficulty in concentrating, or if you become easily startled.

KEY POINTS

- If your anxiety or fear is out of proportion to the threat and causes problems with your everyday life, you are likely to have an anxiety disorder

- Anxiety can result from physical illness and from drugs

- All anxiety problems can be treated

- Anxiety often occurs together with depression

Dealing with anxiety

Four stages to recovery

If you think that you have an anxiety problem there are four stages that you may go through to recovery. You may recover at any stage of this pathway.

1. Visit a GP for a proper diagnosis

Many people find the reassurance of a proper diagnosis enough and either their anxiety symptoms fade or they find ways of dealing with them.

2. Become informed

Read some books on the subject, or join a self-help group through your GP surgery, on the internet or through other recommendation. There are lots of self-help books and programs on the internet and programs that you can obtain for home computer use which may help you to beat your fears (see page 60). It is possible to go it alone but it is a good idea to accept any help or support that is offered. Getting as much information as possible and linking up with a self-help group are important ways of making sure that you stay on the right track. Some people find education and self-help enough to beat their anxiety.

3. Seek help from a therapist
You can find a therapist either through the GP or through one of the organisations listed in 'Useful information' (page 136).

4. Consider other options
If the therapy does not work, consider re-visiting your GP for referral to a specialist mental health unit and consider medication.

Of course if your symptoms are very severe, if you are so distressed that you are considering hurting yourself or if you are too ill to try self-help or therapy, your GP may suggest that you skip some stages and may refer you straight to a specialist unit or offer you medication.

Anxiety and medication
Most people with anxiety problems do not need medication to help them beat their problem. Learning about their problem and being given ways to deal with it are enough to beat it. This does not always work straight away and some people will need a combination of medication and psychological treatment. Different combinations of psychological and pharmacological (medicines) therapies are appropriate for each of the anxiety disorders so, after you have read the chapters on the different treatments, you may want to look at the section that covers your specific problem.

How you can deal with anxiety

Most people's anxiety problems will respond to varying combinations of self-help, psychological and drug treatments to suit the individual circumstances.

Examples of self-help techniques

• Talking to relatives and friends

• Self-help groups

• Computer programs

• Looking after your physical and mental well-being

• Relaxation, for example, yoga

• Complementary therapies

• GP-based self-help

• Bibliotherapy – educating yourself about your condition

Psychological therapies

• Behavioural therapy

• Cognitive therapy

• Cognitive–behavioural therapy

• Counselling

• Hypnotherapy

• Psychoanalysis

Drug (pharmacological) therapies

• Benzodiazepines

• Antidepressants

• Beta blockers

• Buspirone

• Tranquillisers

• Herbal medicines

KEY POINTS

There are four stages to recovery from an anxiety problem:

1. Visit your GP for a proper diagnosis

2. Inform yourself about the condition

3. Seek help from an appropriate therapist

4. If the therapy does not work re-visit your GP to review your options

Management of anxiety disorders using self-help techniques

The value of self-help techniques

There is much you can do to help yourself, which may be useful in reducing anxiety. Do not try to do everything at once. Take it step by step.

Reading this book and others like it will be useful. At the back of this book the useful reading selection includes self-help manuals. They will teach you how to be your own therapist.

Not everybody will succeed with self-help so do not be disheartened if you need more support. If you have a severe problem, you will probably need help. Nobody expects you to do everything by yourself.

Preparing for problems

Anxiety problems often start after a stressful event. If you have anxiety symptoms you may find that they become worse as stressful or emotional events loom. Some stressful events are predictable, such as your children going off to university, a wedding or examinations. To make these events less stressful you need (1) to be open and honest about how stressful they may be and (2) to prepare for them.

If you acknowledge your feelings and talk them over you will feel better. A friend may be able to support you and other people may be more considerate if they are aware of your circumstances. It is not a good idea to shy away from the situation or to do less than you would normally because you would be giving yourself the message that you are not up to managing the situation. The aim should be to work out what support you may need and how you are going to succeed rather than getting other people to do things for you.

Good preparation is important. Read about what you are going to be doing. Plan the strategy properly and try to take commonsense measures to make the situation as stress free as possible.

Self-help groups

Joining a group can be a very useful thing to do. There are a number of charities and self-help organisations that run groups to help people with anxiety problems.

Support and self-help groups may involve face-to-face meetings or telephone conference groups. Some people join internet-based groups. Self-help groups offer advice, support, information and other sources of help. They can help you to understand where your fears and anxieties are coming from and help you challenge them. They can also give you the support to try out new situations and challenges so that you are not imprisoned by worry. Hearing how other people who have anxiety problems are coping with their fears can help encourage you to do the same.

Self-help groups are often run by people who have had the illness and recovered. They have first-hand experience, which puts them in a good position to understand what you are going through.

If you think your anxiety problems may be the result of your marriage you could contact Relate – the marriage guidance council. For problems associated with bereavement you may wish to contact Cruse, the bereavement organisation. See 'Useful information' (page 136).

Computerised help

There are now several computer software packages that have been developed to treat anxiety problems. They can be used at home or in special clinics.

Some programmes are not free and may also need to be prescribed by your GP or specialist. The following website gives a good overall view: www.anxiety.org.uk

OCFighter

This computerised therapy program is designed for people with obsessive–compulsive disorder. It is produced by ST Solutions Limited. It is currently unclear exactly how well this approach works. Best advice would be continue using it if you have already started. But check out the current state of the evidence with your doctor or therapist before you start it.

FearFighter

This is a computerised package that follows the principles of cognitive–behavioural therapy (see page 81). It is also produced by ST Solutions Limited. It is specifically for panic and phobias and helps you set up a programme to identify and challenge the negative types of thinking that keep you anxious. It also helps you to set up a programme of action to fight your fears. The program is available at www.fearfighter.com but it is not free.

Restoring the balance

This self-help CD-ROM is designed to help people with anxiety and depression. It is not suitable if your anxiety is severe. It offers strategies for dealing with problems as well as information. It comes with worksheets and is very easy to use. You have to be well motivated to use it by yourself because the program is designed for clinics where someone is available to support you after you have used it. It aims to help you change the way you think so that you are less depressed. This therapy is not free. You can obtain it by visiting www.mentalhealth.org.uk (Publications Link)

Looking after your health

An important part of any plan to improve anxiety is looking after yourself:

- Focusing on looking after yourself, rather than focusing on your anxiety, can help.

- Try to make sure you keep up with your interests, or even start new hobbies in the evening.

- Make a conscious effort to do what you like doing such as listening to music, going shopping, having a massage or going to a concert or film. If any of these make you anxious, make sure you plan properly but try not to curtail your activities because of fear – if you do, you will teach yourself only to be more frightened.

- Exercise is good for your mental health. You should be able to obtain information on exercise classes from your GP's surgery or the local sports centre. Exercise boosts your mood and makes you feel fitter psychologically as well as physically. It doesn't have to be a strenuous physical sport; going for a walk or a swim can do just as well.

- Active pastimes such as bowling are a good way of doing gentle exercise and getting out and about. If you have not done any exercise for a while make sure that you start slowly.

- Eating regularly and healthily and getting a good night's sleep will all help you cope with an anxiety problem.

Yoga

Exercise is important to keep you mentally balanced and get your body working properly. A healthy body leads to a healthy mind. Yoga includes mental and gentle physical movements to keep your body well toned and supple. The mental and physical control and the breathing exercises used in yoga have been said to be good for anxiety problems. However, like many complementary treatments there is no good evidence that yoga works for anxiety. Yoga can give you the time to think, meditate, stretch and concentrate on other interests rather than your worries, and so in that sense it is likely to be good for you.

Alcohol

One thing to avoid is alcohol: many people with

Getting a good night's sleep

Sleep problems are common in anxiety; however, some people do not sleep well for other reasons. Many people find that if they follow this checklist they can improve their sleep:

- If you sleep late in the mornings, make the effort to get up earlier and see if that helps
- Do not take cat naps during the day
- Read a book before you go to bed to take your mind off your problems
- Go to bed at a similar time every night so your body sets up a rhythm
- Make sure that the bed is comfortable.
- Make sure that your bedroom is not too hot or too cold
- Relaxation exercises may help you go to sleep
- Sexual intercourse before you go to sleep can help you wind down
- Take some exercise during the day but do not exercise just before you go to bed – it can make it difficult to sleep
- Having a heavy meal just before you go to bed can make you feel uncomfortable
- Do not go to bed hungry – you will find it difficult to sleep
- Avoid coffee, tea and cola in the evenings; they all contain caffeine which may keep you awake
- Don't drink alcohol – it helps you go to sleep and then wakes you up prematurely
- If you want a drink make sure it is a warm milky one – this will help you sleep
- Don't smoke before going to bed – nicotine is a stimulant
- If you cannot fall asleep within 30 minutes or you wake up at night and you cannot get back to sleep, don't just lie there, it may make your sleeplessness worse. Get up and read a book or watch television

anxiety problems find that a drop of alcohol makes them feel less nervous. This is true but it will also make you feel more depressed and eventually you will find yourself dependent on alcohol to enable you to live your everyday life. Taking a drink to cure anxiety problems is known to lead to alcoholism and other drinking-related problems. Many people find that the problems they suffer through their use of alcohol are far worse than the problems they experienced from their anxiety – and their anxiety is still present.

Stress management

Reducing stress is important for all of us. We need a certain amount of stress to help us succeed but too much is not good for us.

Learning how to relax properly is important. Many GP surgeries have relaxation groups and this is often a good place to start. Alternatively, you can buy books or tapes that will teach you how to relax. It is easier, though, if you have someone teaching you.

Relaxation classes are covered in the section under 'Psychological treatments for anxiety disorders' (see page 71). There are other methods of relaxation including biofeedback and autogenic training. In biofeedback you are shown how to relax by a machine that monitors your body. In autogenic training you are taught simple mental exercises that help you relax. Both forms of relaxation training initially require the help of a therapist. You can follow the relaxation technique that I use (see box on pages 66–7).

Massage

Massage is another relaxation technique that helps to reduce stress and anxiety levels. It can be done by you, your friends or a professional. There are plenty of devices that can be bought to help you massage yourself, but it is usually easier to ask someone else to do it. Specialist types of massage are good for stress.

Shiatsu
This is a Japanese massage technique based on traditional Chinese medical theory. Our vital life force Qi (or Chi) is believed to flow through our bodies in certain pathways or meridians. If it becomes blocked or there is an imbalance, disease occurs. In Shiatsu massage pressure points are manipulated to unblock or balance Qi.

Reflexology
This is another ancient massage. Different areas of the foot are thought to be linked to certain body systems. Manipulation and massage of these areas are thought to put right any problems that you may have in a particular body system.

Aromatherapy
This uses plant oils and essential oils to aid psychological well-being.

Complementary therapies
Many people these days turn to complementary or alternative therapy. In some countries people go to a complementary therapist before going to see their GP. The problem with many complementary therapies is that there is little or no scientific research to support the claims of effectiveness. This does not mean they do not work, just that there has not been a reliable study that says whether or not they work. A further problem is that they are poorly regulated. You cannot be certain

A simple relaxation exercise

This is a simple method for relaxing. It only takes 20 minutes, maximum.

You can do it in bed, lying on the floor or sitting in a comfortable chair. Make sure that the chair you use supports your neck.

You may want to try it in the evening first time around – some people feel so relaxed that they fall asleep.

Once you've got the hang of it you will be able to do it anywhere without dropping off – unless you want to.

1. Let your whole body go limp. Try to feel as heavy on the bed or in the chair as possible. Let the bed or chair take your weight. Feel heavy, like a sack of potatoes.

2. Put your arms by your side and let them flop down. Let your legs go floppy as well. Let your shoulders drop. Relax all parts of your body from the top down. Feel heavy on the bed or chair.

3. If you have not done relaxation exercises before, you will need to teach yourself how to relax your muscles. Tense the muscle in your upper leg harder and harder until you cannot tense it anymore. Now release it. You will feel the difference between tension and relaxation. Do the same from the top of your body to your toes.

   • Start with the muscles of your eyelids. Close and tense them, then relax them.

simple relaxation exercise (contd)

- Screw up your face, then relax it.

- Clench your teeth and relax again.

- Shrug your shoulders so that they nearly touch your ears, now let them down.

- Tense and release all the different muscles of your arms, chest, stomach, buttocks, legs, feet and toes one by one.

Try to remember how each of the muscles feels when you have released the tension. The way the muscle feels when you have released the tension is how it feels when it is relaxed. That is the feeling that you are aiming for.

4. You will find that your muscles feel less tense than they did when you started. Remember what they feel like now. Once you have got the hang of it and can remember what relaxed muscles feel like, you will not need to tense them before you relax them.

5. When you feel relaxed and limp, slow your breathing down bit by bit. Make it slow and even. Concentrate on your breathing and nothing else. Make inhaling and exhaling take the same length of time: it should be long and slow. If you feel light-headed, stop.

After 20 minutes of these exercises you will feel better and less tense than before.

that the therapist you see is any good even if you believe that the therapy works.

A sensible and practical approach to using them is to make sure that you have seen your GP to make sure that there is no physical cause for your anxiety. If there is not, try to obtain a relevant therapist by recommendation from the GP or someone else you can trust. A complementary therapist linked to a national organisation would be a good choice.

Homoeopathy

This form of medicine is built on the principle that 'like heals like' and that small quantities of a substance are needed to promote healing. For instance though nettles can sting you, nettle extract may be used in treating rashes. The nettle extract is diluted so that very little of it remains in the lotion that you are given. The nettle extract is thought to work by changing the water used in the lotion so that it affects the body's immune system.

Some GPs are homoeopaths and there are some homoeopathic NHS hospitals. It is worth speaking to your GP for advice before visiting a homoeopath and your GP may well be able to recommend you to a homoeopath with a good reputation.

Be careful with over-the-counter homoeopathic cures. Some of them are herbal not homoeopathic and may interfere with other tablets you are taking. Proper homoeopathic treatment requires a consultation with a homoeopath so that they can tailor treatment to your particular situation.

Acupuncture

Acupuncture works on the same principles of Qi that shiatsu massage does. However, rather than relieving blockages and other problems with the flow of Qi by massage, disposable needles are used. Acupuncture is increasingly being used in the UK for the treatment of pain and some GP surgeries have access to acupuncturists who specialise in depression and anxiety. Good studies of its effectiveness in the UK are not available but it has been used for centuries in the Far East.

GP-based self-help

If you see your GP you may be offered a self-help programme. This could include the following:

- Bibliotherapy: written information and a manual that may reduce your anxiety by helping you to understand and change the way you think about certain situations and relationships.
- Information on how to find a support group led by other people with anxiety problems
- Advice on exercise because this has been shown to improve mood.

Bibliotherapy

This is the use of written material to help improve your problems. The written material ranges from educational books and leaflets about mental health problems to therapy manuals. Educational materials may help you understand your problem and so make it less frightening. Therapy manuals allow you to carry out therapy by yourself. You may be able to sort out your problem without seeing a therapist at all. The manuals ask you to carry out tasks or write assignments as part of the programme. There is no completely set structure to bibliotherapy. Some forms are supposed to be used by themselves, others as part of an overall plan with a therapist eventually involved.

KEY POINTS

- Not everybody will suceed with self-help so don't be disheartened if you need more support

- Talking over your problems will help you feel better

- Self-help groups can be very useful

- An important part of any plan is looking after yourself properly

- Alcohol will not cure your anxiety problems

- Complementary therapies can be helpful but it is advisable to see your GP first to ensure that there is no physical cause for your anxiety

Psychological treatments for anxiety disorders

Background to psychological treatments

Psychological treatments are important in all forms of anxiety. Many psychological therapies have been considered useful in treating anxiety. These include counselling, behavioural therapy, cognitive therapy, relaxation techniques and hypnotherapy.

Until the 1950s long-term therapies, such as psycho-analysis, were the most used treatment for anxiety problems but now relatively short therapies – six to twenty sessions over four to six months – tend to be used.

Long-term therapies worked on the assumption that anxiety stemmed from problems in the past that you had not dealt with properly. The shorter therapies work in the here and now. They are not so bothered about the deep-rooted causes of the problems but more about how you deal with them now and what you can do to stop them continuing to trouble you.

What are psychological treatments?

Many people use the terms 'psychological treatments', 'psychotherapy' and 'talking therapies' interchangeably. Here I use the term 'psychological therapies' to cover the whole group of ways of getting better through interacting with others. I use 'talking therapies' where the therapist's input is through discussing your problems.

Psychological therapies include a number of different types of therapy but their basic ingredient is that a personal interaction, either by yourself or in a group with a therapist, helps you to sort out the difficulties that you are having.

The different types of treatment reflect different theories of why your problems arise and different methods for helping you beat your problems. For instance some therapists think that anxieties are the result of urges deep in your subconscious that have not been dealt with and if they let you sit and talk freely you will eventually find your own solutions. Whereas other therapists believe that anxiety is caused by the way that you respond and behave to life's problems – they teach you to respond differently and make you practise doing so between sessions.

The interaction that you have with a therapist or therapy group is often that you discuss your problems, but it does not have to be. In some types of music therapy you express yourself through the music that you play. In some forms of art therapy you express yourself through artwork that you produce and in some types of relaxation therapy you are taught to relax but do not necessarily talk about your problems. Therapy is many things to many people.

What is a therapist?

A therapist is simply someone who delivers a therapy. There are many different types of therapists. Their training is very varied.

- Psychiatrists are trained doctors who specialise in problems of the mind.

- Psychologists are not trained doctors but have a degree in psychology.

- Clinical psychologists are psychology graduates who have taken further training in assessing psychological problems and delivering types of therapy.

- Psychotherapist is a catchall name for someone who delivers a talking therapy. They may be a psychiatrist, a psychologist, a social worker with special training, an occupational therapist or someone who has none of these qualifications but has taken a diploma, degree level or other course in psychotherapy. There are many such courses around and like most things in life they are of variable quality.

Different types of therapists deliver different types of therapy, but, to make the whole thing more confusing still, some therapists offer more than one type of therapy.

There are various schools of psychological therapies and various approaches. A person who calls him- or herself a psychotherapist could be trained in only one type of therapy or could be trained in many different types of therapy.

All of this makes the world of psychological therapies confusing and difficult to navigate.

Which is the best therapy?

There are lots of claims that one type of treatment is better than another and lots of anecdotal tales of wonder cures. Many of the types of therapy that are used do not have good scientific evidence to support them but the effectiveness of some of the main types of therapy, interpersonal therapy, cognitive therapy, cognitive–behavioural therapy and the behavioural therapies, is supported by good research evidence.

Talking therapies are considered by most specialists to be the first treatment of most anxiety problems. They offer a cure for your current problems and sometimes new skills that will help you to combat anxiety in the future.

Different therapies are thought to work in different ways. Often the relationship with the therapist and the opportunity to talk through your problems help to relieve tension; it also helps you to put situations and events in perspective. Some therapies work by helping you to find a way forward through your problems. Some try to decrease anxiety by helping you to understand what is going on in your body and taking back control over what is happening to you. Others neutralise anxiety and fear by preparing you and, slowly, putting you in the situation that you fear most and showing you that you can cope with it. Studies have shown that some types of therapy have an effect on the brain chemicals that cause anxiety, similar to taking anti-anxiety drugs. Therapy seems to normalise the balance of brain chemicals just like drugs do.

The importance of the therapist

Some therapies have more research than others behind them showing that they work. However, there is a difference between what happens in a research study and what happens in the real world. It is possible to choose a therapy that works but a therapist with whom you do not get on or who is not very accomplished, so the outcome may not be as good as expected.

Finding someone who is a competent therapist and a person to whom you can relate is as important as the therapy that you choose.

Finding a therapist
Within the NHS

Different types of therapy for anxiety are available through the NHS. Access to this is usually via your GP. Availability differs widely from region to region.

There are thousands of private therapists offering a wide variety of therapies. The quality of therapy offered is very variable. You do not need a referral from your GP.

If you think you need therapy for an anxiety problem you should visit your GP first and get a diagnosis. You should make sure that your symptoms are caused by an anxiety problem and not by anything else, for instance other tablets that you are taking.

It is safest to obtain a therapist through your GP surgery or a specialist mental health team. Some GP surgeries will have counsellors on site. Others will have direct access to a psychological therapy department in an NHS hospital or community mental health unit, but in some areas they have to send a letter about you to a specialist mental health team to get the OK before you are referred. This can mean that you have to have an assessment by a mental health team (a psychiatrist, community psychiatric nurse, social worker, psychologist or occupational therapist) before you get access to NHS psychological therapy.

In some areas you can get direct access to a mental health team and cut out the GP. In such areas you can find the contact details of the local mental health team through your hospital and get in touch with them direct.

Therapy outside the NHS

In some areas there are waiting lists or very little therapy available on the NHS. If you do not want to wait for therapy it is still worth visiting your GP surgery because they may have information about a good local private therapist.

Many people think that GPs are too busy to bother with their anxieties, or are worried that they will be embarrassed. Others think that access to therapy will be difficult. As a result of this many people try to find a therapist in the same way they would find a plumber – by word of mouth or by the small ads in newspapers and magazines.

This can be difficult. Also you really should visit the GP to make sure that your problems are psychological and not physical. However, if you do not want to visit your GP surgery – say, for instance, because you had had the problem before and know your diagnosis – a good alternative is to look on the websites of national organisations who accredit therapists (see 'Useful information', page 136).

Another alternative is to approach other organisations that offer therapy to which you can get access without referral such as Open Door or Relate – the marriage guidance council. The Samaritans offer telephone therapy for those in crisis.

Private therapy

If you want to obtain a private therapist it is best to get a recommendation from your GP. Whether you get the information from your GP or go it alone it is best to check that the therapist has a nationally recognised qualification for the type of therapy that he or she is offering you and is a member of a professional association. For instance, if a therapist says that he or she is going to offer you cognitive–behavioural therapy you should ask what qualifications that person has in this and you should check out the qualifications in a library or on the web using the section 'Useful information' (page 136).

This is not a foolproof method but should screen out people who are offering treatment for which they do not have a qualification and who are not members of a professional association. Therapists who belong to professional associations generally have to work to strict guidelines and are accountable to that association.

Lastly, the therapist should have proper insurance – professional indemnity – and undergo supervision at least once a month by another therapist to make sure that they keep up standards.

Remember, if it does not go as well as you would like you can always try another therapy or another therapist. If you do not get on with your therapist, do not be afraid to try another one. But you are unlikely to solve any problems if you keep on changing therapists.

Finding group therapy

Group therapies are useful for some anxiety problems. Groups tend to be run by professionals but some of the self-help and voluntary organisations also run groups. They usually have limited numbers – often fewer than

12. Some you can join by yourself but in the case of others your GP will need to refer you. They meet regularly, often weekly, for between one and two hours for three to four months.

Confidentiality

Talking therapies on a one-to-one basis, which you obtain through your GP, are confidential like any other medical consultation. Unless you specifically ask for things not to go in your notes, a therapist will write to your GP with an overview of what happened in the session.

If you go to group therapy, everybody in the group will know what you have said. If you go to a private therapist, none of the information need make its way back to the GP notes. This is good for confidentiality but it does mean that your GP does not know what happened in the sessions and it may be difficult to obtain the information if you ever need therapy again.

Behavioural therapies

This is a group of different therapies all of which work on the same theory – we learn to be afraid of certain events and situations and so, equally, we can learn not to be afraid of them.

They are usually carried out on a one-to-one basis and involve exposure to the anxiety-provoking stimulus until it no longer causes problems. There are many ways of doing this but the usual way is that you will be repeatedly exposed to the stimulus until anxiety or panic subsides.

This is usually done in a systematic way and you will be given help and advice on how to control your anxiety, for example, by breathing techniques. For instance, if you are afraid of dogs, over a number of weeks you will slowly work up from looking at a picture of a dog to a dog being in the same room as you but on a lead with a handler to you eventually stroking the dog without fear. In between there will be a number of steps that are, bit by bit, more challenging – but you will learn to cope with them.

An important factor in the success of behavioural therapy is that you need to be committed to working with the therapist:

- You write down specific goals and revise these as necessary during the course of the treatment.

- The feelings that are experienced as symptoms are identified and specified.

- You are taught a variety of strategies to deal with the anxiety such as deep breathing and other relaxation techniques.

- You are exposed to the anxiety-provoking stimulus in a graded way.

- You are kept in the anxiety-provoking situation until the anxiety subsides – using the strategies that you have been taught to deal with it.

- You teach yourself that you can conquer your fear and that it does not have to lead to anxiety problems.

Behavioural therapies are usually used on an out-patient basis – you go to the therapist or the therapist comes to you. You often see the therapist weekly but you are expected to practise what happened in the session between visits. However, if outpatient treatment does not work, there are some centres that offer residential or inpatient treatment. For outpatients a number of sessions – between six and twenty – are required. Most people are treated in one to four months.

The success of these therapies depends on how motivated you are to succeed and, if you go to a unit, how good the unit is. Good therapy from a good unit works in over 70 per cent of people and its success is maintained for years after stopping.

Behavioural therapy is available through the NHS. The speed with which you are seen will vary from region to region. You can find a properly registered behavioural therapist through the British Association of Behavioural and Cognitive Therapists (see 'Useful information', page 136).

It is possible to set up a behavioural programme of your own, if you are highly motivated, from the internet and computer programs and books.

Cognitive therapy

Cognitive therapy works in a relatively short period of time. You can obtain it on a one-to-one basis or by attending a group. This form of therapy involves getting you to think about the causes of your anxiety and to challenge why they make you anxious.

For instance, a person with panic attacks who fears that he or she is having a heart attack will be asked to challenge the assumptions that make him or her believe this. The therapist will explain how the symptoms are produced and demonstrate that the person does not have a heart problem. The aim is to encourage more logical ways of thinking. This stops the fear reinforcing itself and developing increasing anxiety.

Cognitive therapy may be available from the GP or from a psychiatric unit. Many private therapists now offer cognitive therapy. You can find cognitive therapists through the British Association of Behavioural and Cognitive Psychotherapists (see 'Useful information', page 136).

Cognitive–behavioural therapy

Some therapists combine cognitive therapy with behavioural therapy to produce cognitive–behavioural therapy. Fears and anxieties are attacked from two sides. You expose yourself to your fears and take control of your anxiety very much like behavioural therapy but you also use your brain to challenge why you were afraid of it in the first place and to understand the symptoms that you are feeling.

The therapy involves looking at your problems, examining your thought and behaviour patterns, and working out ways of changing negative thoughts and behaviours that lead to anxiety. You then practise what you have learned in the sessions when you are out and about between sessions.

There is now a lot of research that shows that this sort of therapy works and works well. In six to twenty sessions, lasting fifty minutes a session, most people feel significantly better.

Cognitive–behavioural therapy is available through the NHS. Some GP surgeries and most specialist mental health units will have cognitive–behavioural therapists available. The waiting list is variable. It is possible to find a private therapist but you must make sure that he or she is properly qualified and practising cognitive–behavioural therapy based on well-recognised techniques. There are a number of websites that you can use to find a qualified therapist (see 'Useful information', page 136).

Counselling

Counsellors listen, empathise, act as a sounding board and help people decide on how they are going to solve their problems. If you go to see a counsellor he or she may be non-directive which means that he or she may not try to control what happens in the session or what you talk about, or he or she may be directive which means that he or she tries to identify what is provoking your anxiety with the aim of helping you face this and deal with it.

Counsellors often do not offer answers to people's particular problems. They aim to help you find your own answers. Counselling is often available from the GP surgery. If your GP does not have a counsellor you can find one through the British Association of Counselling website (see 'Useful information', page 136).

Does counselling work? Many people find counsellors helpful but the jury is still out as to whether or not they are particularly effective in the treatment of anxiety. Some specialists do not think that counsellors have a sufficiently rigorous training to deal with serious anxiety problems.

Hypnotherapy

There is a variety of types of hypnosis that are used to treat anxiety. In hypnosis the therapists usually put you in a state of very deep relaxation, which is called a trance. During the trance the problem that is causing the anxiety can be explored and sometimes neutralised. Alternatively, while you are in a trance the hypnotherapist can suggest other more constructive ways in which you can deal psychologically with your worries.

Some therapists make clients imagine being exposed to their phobia during hypnosis and being able to relax and deal with it. Some people like hypnotherapy because it works very quickly. Others say that it does not work for them at all.

It is often difficult to find hypnotherapy through your GP on the NHS, but your GP may know of good therapists in your area. The British Society of Clinical Hypnosis has a list of private therapists. If you join Anxiety UK (previously known as the National Phobics Society), there is a charge for membership, you will have access to their clinical hypnotherapy service (see 'Useful information', page 136).

Psychoanalysis

The aim of psychoanalysis is to sort out long-standing problems. It is not a quick fix; it takes many months and sometimes years. There are many types of psychoanalysis all based on different theories of where problems come from and how they can be resolved.

They all share the view that anxieties, fears and worries are caused by problems from the past that have not been properly dealt with. We may have denied them, ignored them or tried to forget them but they are still nagging away at the back of our minds. They stay there and fester and come back to us when we are under stress or weakened in some way. They may also weaken us, making us more vulnerable to stress.

An example of what could cause problems is the loss of a parent when we are young. If we are too shocked to grieve properly we may just cover up our feelings, but they do not go away and they come back to haunt us in our adult life as stress and anxiety.

Long-term psychotherapy aims to release these bad feelings out into our consciousness. Once they are there, psychotherapy tries to help us disarm the feelings so they stop causing problems.

There are so many different types of long-term therapy available, and so many different people who are happy to offer it, that it is best to contact your GP for a recommendation. Psychodynamic psychotherapy is available on the NHS but there are often long waiting lists.

Despite the fact that psychotherapy has been used for over 100 years there are few good scientific trials that demonstrate that it works to cure anxiety problems.

Relaxation

Learning how to relax is easier said than done. Relaxation is something that most of us need to do and most of us find difficult.

There are many ways to relieve anxiety and learning some of these techniques is useful if you suffer from anxiety. Relaxation classes are often available through the NHS at GP surgeries or specialist centres. Usually group relaxation classes are given. One-to-one sessions are reserved for people with severe anxiety. Group classes can last for anything from one session or more, but are often once a week and last for about a couple of months. A session usually lasts an hour or so.

There are lots of techniques that are taught. One thing that they have in common is that they teach you to recognise when you are tense and how to relieve the tension. If you do not want to go to a group, you can instead buy relaxation tapes.

Other psychological therapies

There are many therapies available that claim to work in anxiety problems. Below are listed some that you may hear mentioned.

Autogenic training

This comprises a set of mental exercises that helps you to relax. You are taught this by a therapist to begin with and then you can do it alone.

Cognitive analytical therapy

This is a relatively new therapy that links cognitive therapy, some behavioural components and some psychoanalytic theory to produce a powerful therapy. There is scientific research that shows it works well but finding a cognitive analytical therapist can be difficult; your GP may be able to help.

Eclectic therapy

This is a name given to the use of more than one type of therapy in a session. Some therapists are trained in a number of therapies and use theories from many of these when they see a patient.

Eye movement desensitisation and reprocessing (EMDR)

This type of therapy rose to fame in the treatment of post-traumatic disorder. The person with the condition recalls the traumatic event while making particular eye movements and this decreases the trauma. Although it may sound far-fetched, there is quite a lot of research to demonstrate that how we remember events and situations depends on the way in which we move our eyes.

Interpersonal therapy

Therapists help you to investigate personal relationships, how to deal with and relate to other people, and how to deal with conflicts and losses in your life. They relate these events to your mood. They offer you explanations for why you feel the way that you do and recent interpersonal events and relationships. These are linked to how they make you feel.

Neurolinguistic programming

It is difficult to categorise this therapy because it has some cognitive and also some hypnotic elements. Neurolinguistic programming (NLP) is usually performed on a one-to-one basis. The number of sessions is variable. It works on the assumption that we programme our brains every day to make sense of the world by using thoughts and images.

Anxiety problems are believed to be the result of faulty programming and can be cured by reprogramming our response to life events and situations.

Whether we think a cup is half-empty or half-full depends on the way we tell our brains to think about the situation. Whether or not we are afraid of spiders is the result of faulty programming because we know at a conscious level that the fear does not make sense.

These fears can be managed by reprogramming and NLP is one way of reprogramming our brains. It aims to help people take control of their thoughts and actions. This is done by the identification of self-defeating thought patterns and helping you replace them with more appropriate ones. The standard types of research evidence are not available. There are no long-term studies that demonstrate how good NLP is, or indeed whether it works at keeping people well. There is little evidence, however, of any harmful effects.

A lot of people vouch that NLP has changed their lives. People like it because it is fast acting. Some NLP therapists claim that they can cure phobias in an afternoon. As a result of this some people with anxiety problems use it before trying other forms of therapy. The assumption is that if NLP does not work they can always move on to a therapy that takes longer and if NLP works they will have saved themselves a lot of time.

NLP is generally not available on the NHS but your GP may be able to tell you of a good therapist in your area.

Rational–emotive therapy
A form of cognitive therapy that challenges negative unwanted emotions and your underlying assumptions.

Systemic therapy
A form of therapy that is usually used for families. The aim is to try to help you with your social network to make you feel less anxious. Your relationships with other people and how you interact are assessed with the intention that everybody will work together to improve the situation.

KEY POINTS

■ Availability of therapy through the NHS is very variable

■ There are many private therapists but it may be difficult to know who is good – you should always check that the therapist has had proper training for the therapy she or he is offering

■ The safest place to obtain a therapist is through your GP surgery or a specialist mental health team

■ Finding someone who is a competent therapist and a person to whom you can relate will give the therapy the best chance of success

■ If a therapy doesn't work for you, after giving it a fair chance, don't be put off trying another therapy

Drug treatment of anxiety

The value of medication

Most people do not need to take drugs to help them overcome their anxiety. Self-help and talking therapies are often sufficient.

If drug treatments are to be used they are best used as part of a management plan that includes psychological therapies. This is because, although drugs can be effective at treating symptoms, they do not usually deal with the underlying causes of anxiety.

In the minority of people where psychological treatments have not been successful, drug treatment alone is warranted.

In the UK, there can be a long wait for a suitably qualified therapist to treat anxiety problems on the NHS. In such cases some doctors prescribe drugs to help alleviate symptoms and allow you to get on with your life. However, some argue that drug treatment can mask symptoms and so make psychological therapy more difficult: if you are not feeling anxiety symptoms, how can they be treated with therapy? Others say that those who have had a quick fix with drugs will be less interested in committing to the hard work that is necessary for some psychological therapies to succeed.

On the other hand, some doctors believe that drug therapy alone, if taken for long enough, can lead to a remission (reduction) in symptoms.

It can be difficult to make a decision on the route that you should take. The most important thing is to talk it over with your GP or a psychiatrist. Next, decide together on a plan of which drugs you are going to take and for how long and what psychological therapy you are going to have and when. Try to stick to the plan.

Types of drugs
Benzodiazepines

The names in the box are the real or generic names, although they also have different names (proprietary/trade names) given by drug companies who sell them. For example, one form of the generic drug lorazepam is also marketed as Ativan.

In the UK benzodiazepines are usually prescribed for only two to four weeks if anxiety is severely disabling, subjecting someone to unacceptable distress. They should not be prescribed for mild anxiety and should be used only for very severe sleep problems.

They work by stimulating the same nerves as the brain chemical gamma-aminobutyric acid (GABA). GABA's role is to decrease anxiety. It makes nerves less excitable.

There are lots of different benzodiazepines. The difference between them is how long their effects last – a drug's effect lasts longer if it takes your body longer to break it down and excrete it.

Examples of benzodiazepines

Benzodiazepines are the most widely used drug for anxiety; they are also used as sleeping tablets.

Benzodiazepines used for anxiety

- Alprazolam
- Chlordiazepoxide
- Clobazam
- Diazepam
- Lorazepam
- Oxazepam

Benzodiazepines used as sleeping tablets

- Nitrazepam
- Loprazolam
- Temazepam
- Flurazepam
- Lormetazepam

Longer-acting benzodiazepines tend to be used for anxiety problems and shorter-acting benzodiazepines tend to be used as sleeping tablets. This makes sense for a number of reasons, one of which is that you want a sleeping tablet to make you feel drowsy at night and help you get to sleep but you want it out of your system by the morning so that you feel fresh and ready to continue with the day. Your body will have got rid of most of the shorter-acting benzodiazepines by the morning, so that you do not wake up with a 'hangover'.

Benzodiazepines treat anxiety symptoms quickly and efficiently. They also produce a mild elevation of mood.

Doctors tend to use these drugs only for anxiety that is severe, disabling and causing extreme distress. Many trials have shown that they are effective in the treatment of anxiety. Although some people use them long term, the evidence is that they tend to work for about four weeks; after this time your body starts to get used to their effects and they do not work as well.

There is little evidence that they are useful long term. An added problem is that, if they have been used for longer than four weeks, there is an increasing likelihood that you may become addicted to them.

People can become dependent on benzodiazepines physically and psychologically and this can make them difficult to stop. Stopping them suddenly produces a withdrawal syndrome, which can be worse than the initial anxiety itself. Some people find that they cannot come off them at all even if they try to come off them gradually.

Another problem with benzodiazepines is that, because they gradually do not work so well, after a few weeks you need more and more of them to achieve the same anxiety-neutralising effect. An initially modest prescription has to be continually increased. The higher the dose the more difficult it is to come off them.

If you have been on a short course of benzodiazepines, they have worked and you have come off them with no problems, they will work again if you need them but it is worth realising that the fact that you need them again is testimony that the problem causing your anxiety has not been sorted out.

Most doctors are wary of the possibility of addiction and the withdrawal symptoms that can occur with this treatment and they are therefore very reluctant to use benzodiazepines long term and they tend to be pre-scribed in short courses while medium to long-term strategies are put in place. Indeed, doctors are warned not to prescribe these drugs for any length of time. Short courses of two weeks of longer-acting agents are preferred.

If nothing else works, doctors may prescribe benzodiazepines for a longer period of time either to try to treat symptoms or to prevent a recurrence of symptoms. However, you should discuss this in depth and make sure that the risks of not using them outweigh the benefits before starting. Before considering long-term benzodiazepines you should have seen a psychiatrist.

If you have been taking benzodiazepines long term and you want to stop, you will need to follow a slow reduction scheme like the one shown in the box.

Reducing your intake of benzodiazepines

- Ask to have your drug changed to diazepam and take this at night. It is easier slowly to decrease the levels of it in the blood, which makes it easier to come off.

- Ask your GP if there is a counsellor available to help.

- With the help of your GP and/or counsellor:
  - reduce the dose of diazepam by 2 to 2.5 milligrams every two to three weeks – if withdrawal symptoms occur, maintain the same dose until they go away
  - reduce the dose by a smaller amount the next time if you have previously suffered withdrawal symptoms
  - continue reducing until you stop completely.

- It does not matter if this takes four weeks or one year – as long as you stop taking the drugs and are all right.

- If there are severe problems the doctor may be able to prescribe a beta-blocking drug that will decrease some of the anxiety symptoms, but will be reluctant to do so because this may complicate matters. If your doctor thinks that you are depressed, he or she may prescribe an antidepressant.

Side effects of benzodiazepines

- Dizziness
- Weight gain
- Menstrual problems
- Drowsiness
- Increased anxiety
- Impaired attention and coordination
- Amnesia
- Difficulty in learning new skills
- Poor memory

Apart from the problem of dependence there are a number of side effects of benzodiazepines. These include dizziness, loss of balance, trouble thinking clearly and sedation which can lead to accidents at home or work. As a result of this you should not drive

Benzodiazepine withdrawal syndrome

Symptoms of withdrawal usually start within two days of stopping the benzodiazepine, but, if you are taking a drug of long duration of action, symptoms may take a week or so to become apparent. The symptoms usually disappear in a few weeks but for some they are so troublesome as to be unbearable. Moreover, in some people their symptoms of anxiety become worse when they are stopped.

Withdrawal symptoms from stopping benzodiazepines

- Anxiety
- Insomnia
- Shakiness
- Hypersensitivity to noise
- Nausea, loss of appetite
- Poor concentration
- Headaches
- Dizziness
- Tiredness

or use dangerous machinery when you are using these drugs. Prescription of benzodiazepines has been associated with a 50 per cent increased risk of hip fractures. This increased risk is in the first few days of being prescribed benzodiazepines and after one month of prescription.

Benzodiazepine as sleeping tablets

Just as in anxiety benzodiazepines work well in helping people sleep, but only for a short period of time. Studies show that they tend to stop working as sleeping tablets after a few weeks. Many people who claim that they still need them to sleep are psychologically dependent on them: relaxation techniques and following the guidelines in getting a good night's sleep (see pages 66–7) are as likely to work. A number of alternative sleeping tablets have been produced including zopiclone, zaleplon, zolpidem and clomethiazole. However, just as with benzodiazepines, the guidance is that they should be used only for relatively short lengths of time.

Antidepressants

Antidepressant drugs are good at decreasing anxiety. Antidepressants have effects on the different brain chemicals that specialists believe are important in producing anxiety symptoms. Different antidepressants work on either different brain chemicals or different combinations of brain chemicals. Serious anxiety is so disturbing that some people become depressed: antidepressants are helpful in that they can treat both the anxiety symptoms and the depression.

Many people who take antidepressants find that their symptoms go away when they take them but come back when they stop them. There is some research that shows that the number of people who have a relapse after they stop their medication can be decreased by staying on the tablets for a year after symptoms have gone away.

However, they are very strong drugs and they can have side effects. Many doctors offer them as their first choice in the treatment of anxiety but some studies show that generally self-help and psychological therapies are better at keeping you well.

Antidepressants may effectively treat your anxiety symptoms. After stopping the medication your symptoms may or may not come back.

Tricyclic antidepressants

These chemicals are called tricyclics because of their chemical structure – three rings that are linked together with a side chain – like a tricycle. Two types of tricyclics, imipramine and clomipramine, have been shown to have some effect in treating some types of anxiety problems. How exactly these drugs decrease anxiety is not clear but it is known that they have an effect on noradrenaline (norepinephrine) and serotonin, two of the chemicals that are significant in the development of anxiety symptoms.

Tricyclics have been used to treat anxiety for years but they are used less now because some say that the newer antidepressants are easier to take and cause fewer, and different, side effects. Older antidepressants are more toxic in overdose than the newer ones and, given that anxiety disorders can be severe enough to lead to depression and suicidal thoughts, this is a material factor justifying the use of newer rather than the older antidepressants.

Tricyclics are powerful drugs and, like all effective drugs, they can have side effects. Not everyone develops side effects but, if you do, tell your doctor. Side effects can be reduced by starting the drugs at low doses and building up. Some people experience more side effects on one tricyclic than another, so trying different medications may be a sensible option.

Tricyclics may interfere with other medications that you take – even hay fever tablets bought over the counter – so you should consult your doctor or pharmacist before taking anything else.

An overdose of tricyclics can be fatal. As a result of this only a small number of pills should be kept at home if someone is suicidal and the medication should be kept well out of the reach of children.

Tricyclics should not be stopped abruptly: they need to be gradually tailed off, otherwise you may

Some side effects of tricyclic antidepressants

- Blurring of vision
- Constipation
- Difficulty getting and maintaining erection and ejaculation
- Difficulty passing water
- Dry mouth
- Irregular heart beat
- Giddiness on standing
- Tremor of the hands
- Weight gain

Withdrawal symptoms from tricyclics

- Chills
- Muscle ache
- Sweating
- Headache
- Nausea
- Difficulty sleeping
- Lots of dreams

experience withdrawal symptoms. These symptoms do not indicate that you are dependent on the drugs. People who are addicted to drugs crave them; they are dependent on the drugs physically and psychologically. Your body needs to become used to not having the drug in the circulation. Slowly coming off the drugs minimises the withdrawal syndrome.

SSRIs

The initials SSRIs stand for selective serotonin reuptake inhibitors. They work by interfering with the chemical serotonin being taken into nerve cells. They have the effect of increasing the serotonin available for communication between nerve cells. There are lots of different SSRIs but not all of them have been licensed for use in anxiety disorders and those that have been passed suitable for use in one anxiety disorder may not be considered suitable for another.

More and more doctors are using SSRIs to treat anxiety problems. Good scientific studies conclude that they are more effective than some benzodiazepines and tricyclic antidepressants in the treatment of anxiety states.

Their principal side effects are nausea, vomiting and sexual problems with erection and ejaculation. Some people find that they are initially more anxious for up to a couple of weeks when they take SSRIs; however, this usually settles down and they eventually make them less anxious. There are some studies that show that a very small group of people find that they get increased suicidal and homicidal thoughts when they take SSRIs; if you find this you should consult your doctor urgently.

The doses used in anxiety problems vary. Often it is considered best to start low and gradually increase the

Some examples of SSRIs

- Fluoxetine
- Fluvoxamine
- Citalopram
- Paroxetine
- Sertraline

Some side effects of SSRIs

- Stomach discomfort
- Diarrhoea
- Nausea
- Vomiting
- Headache
- Restlessness
- Anxiety

dose to the level used in depressive illness. This decreases the risk of side effects.

Most medication should not be stopped abruptly and this is true of most SSRIs. They should be tailed off slowly. If they are stopped suddenly this can lead to a withdrawal reaction (SSRI discontinuation syndrome – see box below), which can be unpleasant. Withdrawal symptoms are not a sign that you are addicted to the drugs. They are simply a reflection of the fact that the drugs are powerful and your body has become used to them. You generally need to stop them slowly so that your body can readjust; however, some SSRIs can be

SSRI discontinuation syndrome

- Flu-like symptoms
- Shock-like sensations
- Dizziness
- Difficulty sleeping
- Excessive dreaming
- Irritability
- Crying spells

stopped abruptly – consult your doctor before stopping your drugs.

Monoamine oxidase inhibitors

Monoamine oxidase inhibitors (MAOIs) are antidepressants. They were the first type of antidepressants to be developed. They work on a chemical called monoamine oxidase which is important in the production of the brain chemicals that are part of the anxiety response.

Unfortunately monoamine oxidase is also important for the breakdown of a substance called tyramine, which is contained within a number of foodstuffs. If you have too much tyramine in your body you can develop high blood pressure and a violent throbbing headache, which leads to a stroke. As a result of this, anyone who is taking these drugs has to follow a strict diet, which is low in tyramine, and they have to carry a card with them.

Examples of MAOIs

- Phenelzine
- Isocarboxazid
- Tranylcypromine
- Moclobemide

MAOI discontinuation syndrome

- Agitation
- Irritability
- Unsteadiness on your feet
- Difficulty in sleeping
- Vivid dreams
- Difficulty in thinking
- Changes in the pattern of your speech
  – talking too much or too slowly

It takes two weeks for the body to make new monoamine oxidase so even when you have stopped taking MAOI drugs you need to stay on the diet. It is also hazardous to take other antidepressants until your body is back to normal.

More newly developed MAOIs are less likely to cause problems. However, you will still be asked to stick to the diet. Similar to antidepressants MAOIs should not be stopped abruptly. If they are stopped suddenly they can cause a discontinuation syndrome.

Other antidepressants
Venlafaxine
Venlafaxine is an antidepressant that has similarities to both the SSRIs and the tricyclics. It is useful in anxiety but can cause a skin rash. This should be reported immediately to your doctor because it may indicate a serious allergic reaction. It can cause problems with skilled tasks. It has similar side effects to SSRIs and can cause withdrawal symptoms if stopped abruptly. There is increasing evidence that this drug is useful in the treatment of anxiety problems and disorders and is used widely for these.

Reboxetine
Reboxetine selectively works on noradrenaline. It has been shown to be a useful treatment in some forms of anxiety. It can have many of the side effects of other antidepressants.

Beta blockers
These drugs block some of the effects of the chemicals – adrenaline and noradrenaline – that produce most of the symptoms of anxiety. They are called beta blockers

because they block a nerve system called the beta-adrenergic nervous system. These drugs do not have any impact on the development of anxiety: they simply treat the symptoms. They are not a cure.

They are useful drugs in the treatment of physical effects of anxiety such as shaking or palpitations. They may also be useful in people with social phobia who are concerned about the possibility of vomiting.

They are used in the UK but not very much elsewhere. This is because they have a number of side effects. They can be particularly hazardous to people who have asthma and can cause dizziness through their effects on reducing blood pressure. If used in very low doses, their side effects should be minimal.

They tend not to cause discontinuation syndromes but as with all drugs they should be stopped only after discussion with your doctor. The drugs are very powerful and should be taken only in the dose that is prescribed.

Examples of beta blockers

- Propranolol
- Oxprenolol

Buspirone

Buspirone affects the action of serotonin, one of the brain chemicals implicated in the production of anxiety. It works as well as benzodiazepines in reducing anxiety. It tends to work much more slowly than benzodiazepines and takes days to a couple of weeks to work rather than working straight away. Once it is working it can work well. There is some evidence that people who have previously been taking benzodiazepines do not have as good a response to buspirone as others.

Buspirone has fewer side effects than the benzodiazepines, the most common being dizziness, nausea and headaches. Some patients find these side effects intolerable and stop taking the medication but four out of five continue.

Buspirone does not seem to cause the same problems with sedation, tolerance or withdrawal problems that have plagued benzodiazepines.

Low-dose major tranquillisers

Some of the drugs used for schizophrenia and other disorders are sometimes used in anxiety disorders. These drugs have an action on many of the chemical pathways in the brain including serotonin pathways. They decrease anxiety but can also make you drowsy. They are commonly used in much lower doses than in schizophrenia. Drugs include flupentixol and the newer drugs are quetiapine and risperidone. Thioridazine is rarely prescribed because of potentially fatal side effects.

All the major tranquillisers have significant side effects such as drowsiness, tremor, heart and liver problems, difficulty in passing water and sexual dysfunction, and they tend to be used only when other drugs do not work. They tend to be used together with other medication, for instance, antidepressants. Data supporting their use are not that good and they should be prescribed therefore only by a psychiatrist.

Herbal medicines
Do they work?

There is a lot of confusion about herbal medicines. Some doctors believe that they do not work because there is a lack of good research data that show that they do. However, because there are few research data it does not mean, necessarily, that something does not work. It often means that no one, yet, has done the formal scientific research. Many herbal medicines have been used for centuries and people have found them effective. This should not be good enough evidence, however, for you to use them.

Are they harmless?

Another area of confusion is that people who use them think that they are herbal, natural and, therefore, by definition, harmless. This is not true. They are often powerful drugs, they have side effects like other drugs and they can have serious effects in combination with other tablets that you are taking or on other illnesses you have. It is a question not only of whether or not they work, but also of whether they may cause harm. For example, if you are thinking of having a baby, you would need to consider whether they may cause harm to an unborn child.

Is herbal medicines' composition regulated?

The real difficulty that doctors have with herbal medicines is that they are considered unpredictable because there is not much scientific information available. As they are not as well regulated as other medicines, it is difficult to know exactly what a patient is taking. Doctors sometimes find it difficult to understand why people will not take drugs that are well researched and very highly regulated and thus preferable to herbal medicines, which are often poorly researched and poorly regulated.

Talk to your GP

If you are thinking of taking herbal medicines for your problems you should talk to your doctor first. You must make sure that the herbal medicine you are thinking of taking is safe for you. Remember that if you are taking herbal medicine you must tell your GP before you start taking any other medicine.

The strength of herbal medicines can be different from brand to brand so it is best to stick to one brand once you have started taking it.

St John's wort

St John's wort contains extracts of the herb *Hypericum perforatum*. There are at least 10 different chemical components in St John's wort and it is unclear which acts in depression and what is the best combination of these chemicals.

Different brands of St John's wort have different balances of the chemicals and are sold in different strengths. They vary in their ability to treat depression and the fact that there are different sorts of St John's wort has made research difficult. It is unclear what the correct dose of St John's wort is for depression.

St John's wort can be regarded as an antidepressant. The work that has been done shows that it probably works very similarly to other antidepressants by affecting the brain chemicals, noradrenaline and serotonin. The scientific data that there are show that it is an effective treatment of mild-to-moderate depression and there is recent research that claims that it can work for severe depression as well. In some European countries St John's wort is the most prescribed antidepressant.

The data on this drug's usefulness as a treatment of anxiety are not so good. In the UK you can buy St John's wort over the counter in chemists, herbal and health food shops: nevertheless, beware, this is a strong drug with side effects. People who are prone to having high and low moods can become very high in mood on St John's wort.

St John's wort interacts with a number of drugs through its effect on the liver where it increases the action of certain chemicals that break down other drugs. Studies have shown that it can decrease the usefulness of some heart drugs, the contraceptive pill, asthma drugs and even drugs used to combat HIV, to name just a

Some side effects of St John's Wort

- Dry mouth
- Nausea
- Constipation
- Tiredness
- Dizziness
- Headache
- Restlessness
- Nerve damage

Drugs with which St John's Wort interacts adversely

- Digoxin – heart medication
- HIV medications
- Contraceptive pill
- Theophylline – asthma treatment
- Ciclosporin – immune system suppressant used in transplant recipients
- Warfarin – anti-clotting drug
- Sertraline – antidepressant
- Paroxetine – antidepressant
- Triptans – used in migraine

few. Life-threatening interactions have been reported with other antidepressants and migraine medication.

If you want to start using St John's wort you should consult your GP or hospital specialist first. If you are taking other medication at the same time as St John's wort, you should consult your GP before you stop it – stopping it may increase the amount of the other drug in your body because taking away St John's wort decreases the actions of the chemicals in the liver that break down other drugs and lead to side effects.

As different brands of St John's wort have different strengths you should also tell your GP if you change the brand you are using. You should not take St John's wort with any other antidepressant unless you have discussed it with a doctor.

Bach flower remedies

These are a complex type of herbal remedies that are available from some pharmacies and health food shops. They come with leaflets telling you what to take for which symptoms and how much to take. The rock rose is suggested for panic and rescue remedy for emergencies. Many people swear by them but there is little scientific evidence that they work.

Kava

This is derived from a pepper plant, *Piper methysticum*. There is good evidence that this extract can reduce anxiety symptoms and help people sleep. The plant is ground up and mixed with water to make a drink. Tablets are also available from chemists. However, although effective, kava is somewhat controversial. There have been reports of severe liver damage caused by kava, which led to it voluntarily being taken off the market. It is still possible to obtain kava, but it is best to discuss using it with your GP and establish what the current safety guidelines are.

Valerian

This is a plant extract with a long history of use. It has been shown to decrease restlessness and help people sleep. It tends not to produce the 'hangover' that some prescribed drugs do. It is available in many pharmacies.

In general, nothing is for nothing in this life. There are very few drugs that work that have no side effects. It is best not to take any drugs for sleep unless you have to. There are relatively few data available on this tablet. It is best to discuss your sleep with your doctor and see if there is anything that can be done before taking a tablet with unknown side effects.

KEY POINTS

■ Anxiety can be effectively treated in a number of different ways, including self-help, complementary therapies, psychotherapy and drug treatments

■ All drugs have effects, some of which are desirable and some of which are not – these latter are known as side effects

■ If one drug does not work or has unpleasant side effects, you may decide to try another drug or, if they are not severe, that you would prefer taking the drug despite the side effects

■ Always inform your doctor of all other medications that you may be taking – including over-the-counter remedies, and herbal and homoeopathic remedies – because of the possibility of drug interaction

■ Most medication should not be stopped abruptly – consult your doctor before stopping your medication

Seeking professional help

When you see your GP

If you have a problem with anxiety, fear or panic you should visit your GP. This is because anxiety is a symptom of physical as well as psychological problems.

Occasionally, severe panic attacks may worry you so much that you want to go straight to an accident and emergency department rather than wait to see your GP. Most accident and emergency departments will have no problem with putting your mind at rest and running a few tests. They will refer you back to your GP for a full assessment and non-urgent tests. It is important that you do what they suggest and see your GP. Even if they give you the all clear and forget to tell you to see your GP, you should nevertheless visit your GP.

A treatment strategy

When you visit the GP he or she should spend some time talking about your personal circumstances, what you do day to day and any medication you are taking.

They will need to assess how anxiety problems are affecting your life and those around you and will also want to assess whether or not you are depressed. It may take more than one consultation and a number of tests to make sure of the diagnosis. Once the diagnosis is made, your doctor or a nurse or therapist, if there is one at the surgery, should sit down with you and discuss a treatment strategy. You should agree a structured plan and discuss how long it will take the treatment to work, how frequently you will be seen, whom you can contact if it is not going to plan and what the options are if the first treatment that you try does not work for you.

There are often different options for treatment that depend on what you want and what is available locally.

- You may desire quick relief from symptoms and therefore prefer to take medication first and try therapy later.

- You may be a person who does not like drugs and so you may want to wait until therapy is available.

- You may be a person who does not like GPs too much or the medical model of treatment so you may obtain a diagnosis and then decide that you would prefer to contact a self-help group.

- You may want to do all of these. Your GP can give you advice but the decision on what you do is up to you. The only thing you should not do is to do nothing.

If you decide on self-help, your GP should be able to give you information on local groups if the GP surgery itself does not run a self-help group.

If you decide on getting therapy you should be able to obtain this without being referred to a specialist.

What you should ask your GP

- How many people with your anxiety problem has he or she treated?
- What is your diagnosis?
- Will you get better?
- How long will it take to get better?
- What can you do to help yourself?
- Is there any information such as leaflets available at the surgery?
- What are the treatment options available at the surgery?
- How long will treatment take?
- Is it worth being referred to someone else for treatment on the NHS or should you try to find someone outside the NHS?

If you decide on taking medication the GP should discuss with you the different options including the risk, for instance, the possible side effects and the questions of overdose and dependence on benzodiazepines.

If you start medication you should see your GP regularly and, if you are not better after three months, you should discuss changing the medication. If you feel better with medication, stay on it for at least another six months.

If you have given both medication and self-help or therapy thorough attempts and your anxiety has not lessened, you should ask your GP to refer you to a specialist, who will see you in a day hospital or a psychiatric outpatient clinic. The specialist will assess the treatments that you have had and set up a treatment plan with you for the future.

KEY POINTS

■ If you have a problem with anxiety, fear or panic you should visit your GP

■ Formulate a treatment strategy with your health-care providers

■ Your GP should be a good source of local information on self-help and therapy

■ If you have given both medication and self-help or therapy thorough attempts without success, ask your doctor to refer you to a specialist

Case studies for specific conditions

Agoraphobia
Case history

Rachel is a mother of two and happily married. She is a busy house-wife. She has been trying to keep the household together by herself and has been looking after her sick father who lives a few minutes away from her. While she was getting groceries from a supermarket she felt suddenly that she could not breathe. She felt clammy and her heart was going quickly. She felt as if she were going to pass out. She went outside, leaving her shopping, and sat on a bench. Once she had gathered her strength she went home and called her husband. Over the next few weeks she found that she would experience the same symptoms every time she left the house. Initially, it happened just in the supermarket but later it happened even as she left home to go to her front gate. She found that she could get her shopping done, but only if her husband took her and stayed with her. She could care for her father only if her husband or one of the children accompanied her and it was at a time when the roads were not busy. Her husband eventually asked the GP to come and see her.

After taking a detailed medical history and arranging for tests, the GP eventually re-visited and told her that she suffered from agoraphobia, a phobic anxiety disorder characterised by fear of going out. Her husband asked if she may be depressed but the GP said that he could find no evidence of that. The GP offered her the name of self-help groups and prescribed paroxetine, an SSRI (see pages 98–100).

The self-help organisations sent some information but Rachel did not want to meet anyone. She was shy and found it embarrassing to talk about her problems even though all the people she had spoken to on the telephone were pleasant.

Two weeks later Rachel said she was less anxious when she went out but she did not like the fact that she felt a bit tired and also unsteady on her legs on the drug. She decided that she did not want to take any more tablets and wanted to try to beat her fears herself. Her GP put her in touch with a cognitive–behavioural therapist from a NHS psychological treatment centre.

The therapist talked through what she was thinking about when she was having a panic attack. Like many people Rachel thought that she was having a heart attack. She said that she knew that this was not true but she could not help but think that. The therapist also showed how she had trapped herself inside by having her husband and her children support her. She needed to face her fears and deal with them and she needed to do this without her husband and daughter. The therapist taught her some relaxation techniques. They sat down and decided what her goal of therapy should be. Rachel wanted to be able to walk to her father's by herself.

In the first session the therapist walked with Rachel across the road. He then repeated this several times, each time staying further and further away from her. By the end of the session she was crossing the road by herself. The next session was a week later. Between the sessions Rachel practised walking across the road by herself. In subsequent sessions she went further afield with her therapist and then practised doing it alone. By session six she had walked by herself to her father's house. She was still anxious but she had taught herself to cope. She stopped seeing the therapist but, as she continued to deal with her anxiety, she asked her husband to do what the therapist did, going with her initially and gradually leaving her more and more by herself. A month later the therapist took a telephone call from the local supermarket. Rachel had made it.

Self-help
There are a number of self-help groups and books on agoraphobia. It is useful to know what is available and what can be done. It is possible to set up your own therapy programme and act as your own therapist but many people find this difficult.

Therapy
All therapies will try to get you out of the house. Behavioural and cognitive–behavioural therapies are often used. They work well in many people.

Medication

Many people with agoraphobia suffer from panic attacks and depression. Both SSRIs (selective serotonin reuptake inhibitors) and tricyclics have been shown to be effective treatments of the symptoms of agoraphobia and have been used in conjunction with therapies. Some believe that therapy works by itself, and therapy with antidepressants as well works better, but antidepressants alone may not cure the problem.

Social phobia
Case history

Peter has had a problem with eating in public for five years. It started at university but has become steadily worse. He has recently been promoted and so he will be expected to take part in business lunches. He dreads this. He worries that he will shake, blush and spill food and drink. If he is ever asked out to eat he refuses, and if he cannot avoid it he makes sure he has a few drinks to calm the anxiety. He has developed a bit of a reputation as a drinker.

Peter went to see his GP. He was given a number of options, including propranolol (beta blocker) to help him stop shaking and an SSRI. He was told he could be referred to a psychiatrist but this could take some time. He decided to try therapy first and got in touch with a behavioural therapist whom he found through a website. They discussed the problem and decided that Peter had to teach himself that he would not shake, if he blushed it would make no difference to anything and that he would not spill anything.

With the therapist Peter set up a hierarchy of situations that he could not face. This started with having coffee in a quiet café, then having coffee in a busy café where people could see him, then drinking orange juice in an empty pub, to drinking orange juice in a busy pub. He was asked to eat in a restaurant by himself before finally joining his therapist for a meal in a busy hospital canteen. He was asked to work on each of these and move on to the next one only when he was comfortable that he could do the last. Each time he went he had to stay at least 30 minutes so that his anxiety would subside before he left. Once he started going to the coffee house he was asked to go every day at least once a day.

It was difficult at first but Peter eventually became used to it and taught himself that he could do it. He stopped seeing the therapist after eight visits. He found that he was less and less anxious when eating in public. Three months down the line he was asked by his company to meet some overseas businessmen from Japan. He was worried and rang his therapist. He was reassured that there should be no problem and he should go. He was anxious at first and considered going back to his old ways and getting drunk but he could not because none of his guests drank alcohol. He managed to let his anxiety subside and completed the business lunch. That was the first of many.

Self-help
A number of self-help groups exist but many people find it difficult to get in touch with them. People find it difficult to go to groups because they have social phobia. If they can get over this they have taken the first step to recovery.

Therapy
Cognitive–behavioural therapy has the best evidence

base behind it. Some people use behavioural techniques: exposure therapy combined with drug therapy – usually antidepressants.

Drug therapy

First-line drug treatment is antidepressants. Most doctors would use an SSRI. The starting dose of medication is the same as in depression but higher doses may be required. Symptoms tend to respond to treatment after about two months. It isn't black and white how long treatment should be continued for, but many specialists will treat with medication for at least a year.

In an emergency some people use benzodiazepines. They may be prescribed so that you can take them when you want to but many doctors do not like doing this because they fear that you will become dependent upon the medication and they know that this will not solve the problem.

If antidepressants and therapy do not work there are other treatments. One is propranolol. This is a beta blocker that removes some of the symptoms of anxiety and can be used for people who suffer from performance anxiety. Another treatment is buspirone. Some people add buspirone treatment to SSRIs and say that it increases their anti-anxiety effect.

Simple phobias

Case history

Amah has had a problem with dogs since she was a child. She remembers being chased by a neighbour's dog when she was seven. She was distraught and frightened. The fear stayed with her. She is now 45 and, if a dog goes past her, even if it is on a lead, she develops severe symptoms of anxiety. She dealt with the problem by avoiding dogs and this did not really inconvenience her until recently when her daughter met someone she wanted to marry – he was blind and had a guide dog. There was no way that she could avoid the dog. She tried to have a garden party so that she could have her prospective son-in-law around without getting too close to the dog, but it did not work. She got so anxious that she could not relax, and she spent almost no time in the garden pretending to have lots to do in the kitchen. She decided to take on her phobia.

She could not find a local support group and so went to her GP for advice. She was referred to the local NHS psychology service. A junior psychologist there interviewed her. He discussed the body changes that occur during fear and anxiety and taught her ways to relax and get rid of her panic. Between them they set up a graded programme of exposure. The aim was to get to the point where she could pat a dog again. The programme started with looking at pictures of dogs, went on to having dogs in the next room, then in the same room on a leash but a long way away, and then getting gradually closer to a dog until eventually she would touch the dog while it was on the leash. At each stage, over a number of weeks, Amah had to stay with the dog until her anxiety had subsided. She needed to use her relaxation exercises to make sure that she did not get too anxious. The therapist was in the room with her at all times. Finally, it came to the day when Amah had to pat the dog. She watched the therapist do it and then with a lot of encouragement she finally touched the dog.

Unfortunately, the dog got nervous and barked, which made Amah anxious again. She needed more sessions with the dog to build up her confidence.

Within a couple of months she was sitting down to dinner with her daughter, the prospective son-in-law and his dog.

Self-help

Self-help groups, for instance the Triumph Over Phobia groups (see www.topuk.org and 'Useful addresses', page 136) are excellent. Setting up a self-help programme is relatively easy and can be effective if you are committed. Book, telephone or computer-based therapy is effective.

Therapy

Behavioural and cognitive–behavioural therapy has a good track record. Exposure to your fear is important, as is the ability to understand what is happening in your body and take control over it.

Medication

This is best avoided because it does not cure the problem. In extremis a doctor may prescribe a benzodiazepine or a beta blocker to decrease the symptoms of anxiety but this is not common.

Obsessive–compulsive disorder (OCD)
Case history

Paul had a disabling obsessive–compulsive disorder for eight years before he got proper treatment. His fear was that he had left something in the house unlocked and so thieves could get in. His compulsion was checking all the locks. He had a routine for checking that all the windows were locked and had five different types of lock on his front door. They all had to be closed in a certain sequence, starting from the top of the house, and they all had to be locked, unlocked and locked again so that he was sure that he had done it properly. If he was interrupted, broke the routine or was worried that he may not have done all of them properly, he had to start all over again. On a bad day it took him over two hours to get to bed at night and the same to leave the house in the morning. He had recently lost another job because he was persistently late and went to see his GP.

The GP diagnosed Paul as suffering from depression and anxiety as well as OCD and started him on an SSRI (selective serotonin reuptake inhibitor). In the meantime he said he would contact the local psychology and psychiatric departments to see whether he could get further help. On the return visit three weeks later, Paul had stopped the SSRI because he had stomach problems with it and was feeling more anxious because he thought that the GP would not be able to help him. The GP prescribed a short course of diazepam, which made Paul feel much less anxious. It did not completely get rid of his fears or compulsions but made them easier to deal with. When Paul returned two weeks later he got some bad news from his GP: first, the GP would not prescribe any more diazepam because he was worried that Paul would become addicted; second, there was no local treatment and the waiting list for behavioural–cognitive treatment at a national NHS unit in London was many months.

Over the next few weeks his OCD was the worst that it had ever been – he was seriously considering suicide. He telephoned a friend who got the GP to see him at home. The GP persuaded him to attend a local psychiatric outpatient unit. They offered him clomipramine, an antidepressant, and saw him regularly.

Over the next six weeks the clomipramine decreased the OCD, anxiety symptoms and depression. Although it did not get rid of his symptoms completely, he got his checking down to an hour at night and half an hour before leaving the house. He was not suicidal or depressed. He found a job. In general his life was more settled than it had been for some time.

Months later Paul was finally seen at the specialist unit. They took a long history and one of the therapists went to his home with him to see his routine. They talked through his fear and set up a dual action programme. He was going to have to take on his fear psychologically and practically, to challenge the basis of his fear and the assumptions that he made, and slowly to decrease his checking and stop himself from doing too much. Just thinking about doing this made Paul much more anxious. He thought that he had already reached the limit of his willpower. He talked with his friends and family and came to the conclusion that he was the best he had been for ages, less depressed, not suicidal and getting his life back together. He decided that he could control his problems and he did not have the energy for therapy. It was agreed that he could get back to them if he changed his mind.

Self-help
Self-help for this condition is possible but best done through a group.

Therapy
Behavioural therapy and cognitive–behavioural therapy have both been shown to be successful. Therapy seems most effective when linked with drug treatment.

Medication

Many different drugs have been tried which may imply that none is very effective. SSRIs are usually tried first. The tricyclic, clomipramine, has been used for years and has data showing that it works. If these drugs do not work well, a number of other drugs, including the benzodiazepine, clonazepam, has been used and also buspirone. Two antipsychotic drugs, quetiapine and risperidone, have been tried, each of them together with an antidepressant. There seems to be some improvement in the efficacy of the antidepressant at reducing anxiety but there are increased side effects.

Generalised anxiety disorder
Case history

Gillian had been suffering from anxiety symptoms for as long as she could remember. She said initially she had always thought that she was just a pessimistic person because she was always worried about what would go wrong rather than what would go right. She would wake up every morning with the feeling that something was going to go wrong and all day she would be tense and her stomach would churn. She would also think over and over about things that had gone wrong in the past. She felt guilty because of this and because her family played down all her symptoms and asked her to pull herself together. She tried to pull herself together with alcohol which only made things worse – it was another thing to feel guilty about.

When she went to the GP she explained that she had no enjoyment at all in life. She never felt relaxed and her anxiety spoilt everything that she did. Her GP took a thorough history and examined her and then explained that her condition was not life threatening and so she would not be considered a priority by the local NHS services. He referred her to them but also offered her antidepressant drugs. Gillian's view was that she was being offered one type of drug, an antidepressant, to make up for the other type of drug that she was already using – alcohol. She bought books on anxiety, and found a web-based support network and a local group for people with the same problem. She learned how to recognise the symptoms of anxiety such as tensing her shoulders up and learned simple techniques to help her relax.

Her group encouraged her to get her husband to read the books that she obtained and he started to discuss the problem with her family, who became more supportive. Her anxiety symptoms decreased and became tolerable. She decreased her alcohol intake. The NHS therapy seemed to be taking too long so her family decided to pay for a private therapist, who used a cognitive–behavioural therapy approach. At the end of three months of challenging her fears, understanding where they came from and practising stopping thoughts that provoked anxiety, she felt more in control and was enjoying life.

Self-help
Self-help using a voluntary sector group or through the GP surgery is useful. Understanding the problem using information resources from other people can decrease your anxiety. The support of others is important.

Therapy
Relaxation training and anxiety management are effective in reducing symptoms. There is scientific evidence that cognitive–behavioural therapy is useful and in many instances it will be the therapy that is first offered.

Medication

SSRIs are often the first drug that doctors will offer. In generalised anxiety SSRIs take some time to work. Worse still, initially they may make anxiety worse for a week or two. It is worth sticking with them because after one to two months they do work in the vast majority of people. Most doctors start treatment very low, perhaps half the initial dose used in depression, and the dose is increased slowly into the normal range for the treatment of depression. It is unclear how long treatment should be given for. Some state that six months of treatment at least is needed before they are tailed off. If, however, anxiety returns they can be started again.

If SSRIs are not effective many doctors will suggest that you use venlafaxine. It works like an SSRI but is slightly different, and there is good evidence that it works. The dose that is prescribed is low. An alternative is a tricyclic antidepressant. The two most commonly used tricyclics are imipramine and clomipramine.

If antidepressants are not effective in your case there are many other drugs that can be used and their use is supported by research. These include buspirone: it has a delayed onset of action and some people use it in conjunction with antidepressants although it is licensed for use by itself. Beta blockers such as propranolol are sometimes used to calm the physical symptoms of anxiety and the sedative antihistamine (hydroxyzine) is also sometimes used. The latter is only for short-term use; more research is needed into it and it is prescribed only by specialists (psychiatrists).

Most specialists agree that treatment with benzodiazepines should only be short term: this is because they may cause dependence and do not solve the problems that are causing the anxiety. When you stop them you may be as anxious as when you started.

Panic disorder
Case history

Surinder had his first panic attack after a friend died. He can remember it vividly. He thought he was going to die. He talked to his brother and from the reaction he got he believed that his brother thought that he was going mad; he felt isolated and ashamed. He took time off work because he thought he was under stress. He was getting panic attacks at least twice a week and they came out of the blue. He had a panic attack during a visit from his squash partner. He felt that he had to explain what was going on. Surprisingly, his squash partner knew someone who had suffered anxiety problems in the past and knew a lot about them. His friend had been helped by a cognitive–behavioural therapist, and suggested that Surinder look at one of the national websites to obtain more information and that he himself would find the name of the therapist because she had done a good job.

Once he had read the website and the self-help book, Surinder called his friend again and said that he was going to beat his panic attacks by himself. His squash partner persuaded him first to visit his GP. His GP talked through the problems with him, did some tests and said that she could find no physical cause for his symptoms. Surinder decided that he would learn how to relax and focus on the thought, 'Nothing bad is going to happen; this will pass'. When next he got a panic attack he tried to do this. It worked partially – the panic attack did not last as long. From his reading he felt that this was because he was focusing on something else rather than on his symptoms. Two days later he had another panic attack. He again tried his technique. Perhaps buoyed by his previous partial success he was more confident, so the panic attack was shorter still. It did not work every time but over the next month he found that his panic attacks became shorter and much less frequent.

Self-help
Self-help is possible and there are many groups that can support you. Your GP may have a self-help group that can offer reassurance, support and information about panic attacks. This could help you conquer them.

Therapy
Cognitive–behavioural therapy (CBT) and anxiety management and relaxation have all been shown to be useful. CBT is considered by some to be the best treatment for panic attacks and can be combined with drug treatment.

Medication
SSRIs are considered the drugs of choice. Usually, lower doses of SSRIs are used in panic disorder than in generalised anxiety. However, when paroxetine is used, the dose that is used tends to be higher. The effect of the drugs may be delayed and some people's symptoms become worse before they get better. It is unclear how long treatment should be continued. It should certainly be for at least six months but some specialists recommend eighteen months. This is because at least 50 per cent of people relapse when medication is stopped within a few months.

Other antidepressants are also considered useful, and they include the two tricyclics, imipramine and clomipramine, and also reboxetine.

Some doctors use monoamine oxidase inhibitors (MAOIs) and others use drugs usually prescribed for epilepsy but this is not standard treatment.

Benzodiazepines are used by some doctors in emergencies, but this does not seem rational because many panic attacks would have finished by the time the drug gets into the body and is working.

Post-traumatic stress disorder
Case study

Karl was attacked at knifepoint while waiting for a night bus home in London. He initially struggled and one of the three men cut his arm and tried to stab him in the chest, before stealing his wallet and his bag, which contained an important demo tape. He came to the GP surgery six months later. He said that he was OK for a while afterwards and even joked that he had had a lucky escape. He had seen someone from a 'victims of crime group', but did not think that he needed any help. A few weeks later he had stopped being able to sleep and had nightmares. He felt depressed and very anxious, and when he went past a bus stop he sometimes found himself petrified with flashbacks to the incident. He was so anxious that if he saw three men together he sometimes had to leave meetings. His wife said that his personality had changed: he was bad tempered and more aggressive.

He went to his GP, saying that he thought he had post-traumatic stress disorder, and not surprisingly his GP agreed. He was offered either a course of antidepressants or the possibility of waiting until he was seen at a London traumatic stress clinic. Karl's wife convinced him to try to take antidepressants while he was waiting and arranged for Karl to get some counselling. The counsellor offered support but not really any therapy. The antidepressants made Karl feel less depressed but he was still having flashbacks and felt very anxious.

He was seen after some months at the traumatic stress clinic. They allowed him to talk through the incident. He remembered in detail what had happened. He talked through his anxieties and fears. They also set a programme to deal with his depressive thoughts and the fact that he was now avoiding certain situations, which included challenging his fears, making a list of supporting facts and of facts that did not support ideas that he had. It also included stopping himself leaving situations where three men were present. He agreed slowly to build up to going to a bus stop and taking a bus, but refused to do this at night. It took three months of weekly sessions but at the end of it he was less depressed, able to take a bus during the day and able to sleep at night. His next target was slowly to come off the antidepressants over the next two months.

Therapy

Debriefing directly after an incident has its supporters and its detractors. Many doctors think that it is best to wait, to let people use their own coping mechanisms and to wait to see who has a problem. Those who have problems can be effectively treated with anxiety management, CBT and counselling. Some people swear by eye movement therapy (see page 85).

Medication

In post-traumatic disorder low doses of SSRIs are used initially and gradually increased. Sometimes high doses of these antidepressants are needed for the full effect. It takes at least six weeks for the drugs to work and it is not clear for how long treatment should continue. If treatment is continued for six months, only five per cent of people will relapse.

Tricyclic antidepressants can also be used to relieve symptoms and there are good data supporting their use, but less good data for the other medications. MAOIs and drugs used in epilepsy have been tried in some specialist centres.

KEY POINTS

■ Anxiety is common and widespread, as one can deduce from the large number of self-help therapies and support organisations that exist (see 'Useful information', page 136)

■ Your GP will be familiar with anxiety disorders, and will not think less of you; he or she is prepared to help you

■ GPs recognise that anxiety is just as debilitating and threatening to quality of life as a physical illness

■ Non-drug treatments are effective in treating most anxiety disorders and can be used alone or in combination with drugs

Family and friends

Suffering from an anxiety disorder is difficult and painful. Watching a close friend or family member with such a problem is distressing and anxiety problems put a strain on the family. When someone in the family has severe anxiety problems, social engagements, planning and the household routine are all affected. Those suffering from anxiety feel guilty, family and friends sometimes get annoyed and this leads to a bad feeling, all of which can make the problem worse. Everybody is under pressure and can end up pulling in different directions rather than pulling together.

There are some simple practical things that friends and families can do to support someone with an anxiety disorder:

- First, if you think that the person is suffering from such a problem, try to encourage him or her to see the GP and get a diagnosis. But do not force the person to do this if he or she does not want to.

- Next try to learn as much as possible about the specific problem – not because you are going to be his or her therapist but because you won't know how to support the person if you have no understanding about what he or she is going through.

- Make sure that you know what the sources of help are in the area. Where would you need to go in an emergency? Are there any support groups?

- Try not to fall into the pitfall of being too helpful, so hampering the person's recovery. For instance, if you are supporting someone with agoraphobia and you take him or her out all the time he or she may become over-reliant on you.

- Be as flexible as you can while trying to maintain as normal a routine as possible. The aim is to try to make sure that everyone gets what they need and that everything is not distorted by the anxiety problem, but that as much as is reasonable is done to help the person whom you are supporting.

- Do not change things too much. Try to keep to a set routine. Avoid surprises and do not let the person you are supporting down.

- Try to be positive, even about minor achievements. Anxiety is usually beaten step by step. It does not matter how small the steps are as long as they are in the right direction.

- Be careful not to try to take control of everything and to dictate the pace of recovery. If you push someone to do too much too soon, he or she may get worse. Let the person whom you are supporting set the pace. Although you may have read everything there is to know about the problem, you are not suffering from it and the person whom you are supporting will generally know what is needed better than you, so keep talking and checking out whether you are doing what he or she wants.

- Look after yourself. You are no good to anyone if you start getting stressed. Make sure that you have support yourself. Do not take on more than you can manage and make sure that there is appropriate professional back-up for when it is needed.

- Watch out for deterioration, signs of depression, alcohol use and suicidal thoughts. Make sure, if you are worried, that you have discussed this with the person whom you are supporting and with his or her GP or therapist.

Useful information

Useful addresses

Anxiety UK (formerly the National Phobics Society)
Zion Community Resource Centre, 339 Stretford Road
Hulme, Manchester M15 4ZY
Tel: 0844 477 5774 (Mon–Fri 9.30am–5.30pm)
Website: www.anxietyuk.org.uk

Our primary aim is to promote the relief and
rehabilitation of persons suffering with anxiety
disorders through information and provision of self-
help services. To advance awareness of the general
public in the causes and conditions of anxiety disorders
and associated phobias.

ASH (Action on Smoking and Health)
First floor, 144–145 Shoreditch High Street
London E1 6JE
Tel: 020 7739 5902
NHS Helpline: 0800 169 0169
Website: www.ash.org.uk

National organisation with local branches. Campaigns on anti-smoking policies. Offers free information on website or for sale from HQ. Catalogue on request.

Association for Postnatal Illness
145 Dawes Road
London SW6 7EB
Tel: 020 7386 0868 (Mon–Fri 10am–2pm)
Website: www.apni.org

Offers help and advice for sufferers and families affected by postnatal illness. Network of local contacts.

Benefits Enquiry Line
Freephone: 0800 882200 (8.30am–6.30pm weekdays)
Minicom 0800 243355
N. Ireland 0800 220674
Website: www.dwp.gov.uk

State benefits information line for sick or disabled people and their carers.

Bipolar UK (MDF The Bipolar Organisation)
11 Belgrave Road
London SW1V 1RB
Tel: 020 7931 6480
Website: www.bipolaruk.org.uk

Offers support, via self-help groups, to enable people affected by bipolar disorder/manic depression to take control of their lives. Has a 24-hour legal advice line, travel insurance and life assurance schemes, self-management training and employment advice.

British Association for Behavioural and Cognitive Psychotherapists
Imperial House, Hornby Street
Bury BL9 5BN
Tel: 0161 705 4304
Website: www. babcp.com

Professional body providing lists of accredited members to the public.

British Association for Counselling and Psychotherapy (BACP)
BACP House, 15 St John's Business Park
Lutterworth LE17 4HB
Tel: 0l455 883300
Minicom: 01455 550307
Textphone: 01455 550243
Website: www.bacp.co.uk

Professional services organisation and directory of professional counsellors. Offers lists of all levels of counsellors and can refer to local specialist counselling services.

British Complementary Medicine Association
PO Box 5122
Bournemouth BH8 0WG
Tel: 0845 345 5977
Website: www.bcma.co.uk

Multi-therapy umbrella body representing organisations, clinics, colleges and independent schools, and acting as the voice for complementary medicine. Offers lists of qualified and insured practitioners of complementary medicine.

British Psychological Society
St Andrew's House, 48 Princess Road East
Leicester LE1 7DR
Tel 0116 254 9568
Website: www.bps.org.uk

Professional body representing chartered psychologists
and offering lists of qualified practitioners in your area.

Childline
NSPCC Weston House, 42 Curtain Road
London EC2A 3NH
and
Freepost NATN 1111
London E1 6BR
Tel: 020 7650 3200
Helpline: 0800 1111 (24 hours a day)
Textphone: 0800 400222
For children living away from home, or who have been
in hospital for a long time: 0800 884444 (Mon–Fri
3.30–9.30pm; Sat, Sun 2–8pm)

Provides a free and confidential service for children and
young people in trouble or danger 24 hours a day,
every day. Comforts, advises and protects and, where a
child is in danger, works with other helping agencies to
ensure the child's protection.

Cruse Bereavement Care
PO Box 800
Richmond TW9 1RG
Tel: 020 8939 9530
Helpline: 0844 477 9400
Website: www.crusebereavementcare.org.uk

Offers information and practical advice, sells literature and has local branches that can provide one-to-one counselling to people who have been bereaved. Provides training in bereavement counselling for professionals.

Depression Alliance
20 Great Dover Street
London SE1 4LX
Info pack request line: 0845 123 2320
Website: www.depressionalliance.org

Offers support and understanding to anyone affected by depression and for relatives who want help. Has a network of self-help groups, correspondence schemes and a range of literature; send an SAE for information.

Depression UK
c/o Self Help Nottingham, Ormiston House
32–36 Pelham Street, Nottingham NG1 2EG
Website: www.depressionuk.org

Organisation run as a source of support for sufferers from depression, complementary to professional care. Membership offers newsletters, and pen-friend and phone-friend schemes.

Home-Start UK
The Home-Start Centre, 8–10 West Walk
Leicester LE1 7NA
Helpline: 0800 068 6368
Website: www.home-start.org.uk

Trained volunteers, usually parents themselves, offer support and practical help in the home to families with pre-school children for a couple of hours a week in local communities throughout the UK and British Forces in Germany and Cyprus.

Mental Health Foundation
Colechurch House, 1 London Bridge Walk
London SE1 2SX
Tel: 020 7803 1100
Website: www.mentalhealth.org.uk

Offers information and help to survive, recover and prevent mental health problems. Undertakes research, influences policy, and designs training courses for health professionals, sufferers and carers.

MIND (National Association for Mental Health)
Granta House, 15–19 Broadway
London E15 4BQ
Tel: 020 8519 2122
Information line: 0300 123 3393
Website: www.mind.org.uk

Mental health organisation working for a better life for everyone experiencing mental distress with drop-in centres, counselling, advocacy, employment and training schemes. Special legal service for the public, lawyers and mental health workers. Has interpretation service for 100 languages. Offers support via local branches.

National Childbirth Trust
Alexandra House, Oldham Terrace
London W3 6NH
Tel: 0870 770 3236
Helpline: 0300 330 0700
Website: www.nct.org.uk

Self-help organisation offering education, support and advice before and after birth through local groups. Breast-feeding line 0300 330 0772 available 7 days a week 9am–10pm with breast-feeding counsellors.

National Council of Psychotherapists
PO Box 541
Keighley BD21 9DS
Tel: 0845 230 6072
Website: http://thencp.org

Association of therapists, mainly in private practice, to whom the public may confidently refer.

National Family Mediation
Margaret Jackson Centre, 4 Barnfield Hill
Exeter EX1 1SR
Tel: 0300 4000 636
Website: www.nfm.org.uk

Umbrella for 60 non-profit-making family mediation services in England and Wales offering help to couples, married or unmarried, who are in the process of separation or divorce.

National Institute for Health and Clinical Excellence (NICE)
MidCity Place, 71 High Holborn
London WC1V 6NA
Tel: 0845 003 7780
Website: www.nice.org.uk

Provides national guidance on the promotion of good health and the prevention and treatment of ill health. Patient information leaflets are available for each piece of guidance issued.

Nexus
6 The Quay
Bideford EX39 2HW
Tel: 01237 471704
Website: www.nexus-uk.co.uk

An association of unattached people – not a helpline – looking to widen their social lives. People can be referred to groups in their areas.

NHS Direct
Tel: 0845 4647 (24 hours, 365 days a year)
Website: www.nhsdirect.nhs.uk

Offers confidential health-care advice, information and referral service. A good first port of call for any health advice.

No Panic
Unit 3, Prospect House, Halesfield 22
Telford TF7 4QX
Tel: 01952 680460

Helpline: 0808 138 8889 (10am–10pm 365 days a year)
Website: www.nopanic.org.uk

Offers information, support and one-to-one counselling by trained volunteers to people affected by anxiety disorders.

Obsessive Action
Suite 506–509 Davina House, 137–149 Goswell Road
London EC1V 7ET
Tel: 0207 7253 5272
Helpline: 0845 390 6232
Website: www.ocdaction.org.uk

Offers advice on where to go to get help. Has written information, videos and CDs.

Quit (Smoking Quitlines)
63 St Mary's Axe, London EC3A 8AA
Helpline: 0800 002200 (Mon–Fri 9am–8pm,
Sat 9.45am–6pm, Sun 10am–6pm)
Tel: 020 7469 0400
Website: www.quit.org.uk

Offers individual advice on giving up smoking in English and Asian languages. Talks to schools on smoking and pregnancy and can refer to local support groups. Runs training courses for professionals.

Relate (Marriage Guidance) HQ
Premier House, Carolina Court, Lakeside
Doncaster DN4 5RA
Website: www.relate.org.uk

Offers relationship counselling via local branches. Relate publications on health, sexual, self-esteem, depression, bereavement and re-marriage issues available from bookshops, libraries or via website.

Release (Drug-related problems)
124–128 City Road
London EC1V 2NJ
Tel: 020 7324 2989
Helpline: 0845 450 0215
Website: www.release.org.uk

Offers information about problems with prescriptions, and to users and their families and friends.

National helpline ASK FRANK
Helpline: 0800 776600 (24 hours)
Website: www.talktofrank.com

Government helpline offering information and literature on problems with prescriptions and drugs and list of local clinics.

RETHINK (National Schizophrenia Fellowship)
89 Albert Embankment
London SE1 7TP
Tel: 0300 5000 927
Website: www.rethink.org

Campaigns on behalf of people with mental illness and works with the statutory sector. Offers information on severe mental illness to sufferers, carers and professionals. Provides a wide range of community projects, support housing, day services, residential care and respite centres.

Royal College of Psychiatrists
17 Belgrave Square
London SW1X 8PG
Tel: 020 7235 2351
Website: www.rcpsych.ac.uk

Professional body holding lists of qualified psychiatrists.
Patients must be referred by GPs. Publishes factsheets,
books and patient leaflets on mental health problems.

SAD Association
PO Box 989
Steyning BN44 3HG
Tel: 01903 814942
Website: www.sada.org.uk

Offers support and information on seasonal affective
disorder and details of light therapy and equipment.
Enquiries by letter welcomed. SAE requested plus
cheque/postal order for £5 for information pack.

Samaritans
The Upper Mill, Kingston Road
Ewell, Surrey KT17 2AF
Tel: 020 8394 8300
Helpline: 0845 790 9090 (365 days a year)
Website: www.samaritans.org

Offers confidential 24-hour telephone support 365 days a
year to people who feel suicidal or despairing and need
someone to talk to. Local branches listed in telephone
directory; most also see visitors at certain times of the day.

SANDS (Stillbirth and Neonatal Death Society)
28 Portland Place
London W1B 1LY
Tel: 020 7436 7940
Helpline: 020 7436 5881 (Mon–Fri 9.30am–5.30pm;
Tues, Thurs 6–10pm)
Website: www.uk-sands.org

Offers information and support, via local self-help
groups and email, to parents and their families whose
baby has died before, during or shortly after birth. Also
offers support and training to health-care professionals.

SANE
First Floor, Cityside House, 40 Adler Street
London E1 1EE
Tel: 020 7375 1002
Helpline: 0845 767 8000
Website: www.sane.org.uk

Offers emotional and crisis support to people with
mental health problems, their families and friends, and
also information for professionals and organisations
working in the field. Has database of local and national
services.

Terrence Higgins Trust
314–320 Gray's Inn Road
London WC1X 8DP
Tel: 020 7812 1600 (switchboard)
Helpline: 0808 802 1221
Website: www.tht.org.uk

Leading HIV charity offering information, advice and support to anyone who is at risk, living with or affected by HIV.

Triumph Over Phobia (TOP UK)
PO Box 3760
Bath BA2 3WY
Tel: 0845 600 9601
Website: www.topuk.org

Structured self-help groups for phobia and obsessive–compulsive disorder sufferers. SAE requested for further information.

Victim Support
Hallam House, 56–60 Hallam Street
London W1W 6JL
Tel: 020 7268 0200
Supportline: 0845 303 0900
Website: www.victimsupport.org.uk

Refers people to local groups in the UK who offer emotional and practical support to victims of crime and those affected by crime.

Yoga Biomedical Trust
31 Dagmar Road
London N22 7RJ
Website: www.yogatherapy.org

Offers information on yoga therapy to help people with a wide range of medical conditions. Also offers training in yoga therapy and carries out research.

Useful websites

Bodytalkonline
www.bodytalk-online.com
Series of online presentations about different medical conditions.

British National Formulary
www.bnf.org
Has all the information you need to know about different types of drugs prescribed by doctors.

Compassionate Friends
www.tcf.org.uk
Helpline: 0845 123 2304 (10am–4pm and 7–10pm 365 days a year)
Befrienders who offer information and support to parents, siblings and close family members who have lost a child. Support groups locally run by people who have themselves been bereaved.

Healthtalkonline
www.healthtalkonline.org
Website of the DIPEx charity.

Institute of Psychiatry
www.iop.kcl.ac.uk
A national centre for research and the treatment of anxiety disorders.

Patient UK
www.patient.co.uk
Patient care website.

Psychnet-UK
www.psychnet-uk.com
Mental health and psychiatry online magazine.

Stigma-org
www.stigma.org
Campaigning website aimed at fighting stigma and discrimination for those who suffer from mental health problems.

Social Anxiety UK
www.social-anxiety.org.uk

Books

L. Baer, *Getting Control*, 2000.

L. Baer, *The Imp of the Mind*, 2002.

G. Butler, *Overcoming Social Anxiety and Shyness: A self help guide using cognitive behavioural techniques.* Constable & Robinson, 1999.

P. Groves, I. Pennell, *The Consumer Guide to Mental Health.* Harper Collins, 1995.

Christine Ingham, *Panic Attacks*. Harper Collins, 2000.

H. Kennerley, *Overcoming Anxiety: A self help guide using cognitive behavioural techniques.* Constable & Robinson, 1997.

L. Knight, *Talk to a Stranger: A consumer's guide to therapy.* Fontana Collins, 1986.

I.M. Marks, *Living with Fear: Understanding and coping with anxiety.* McGraw-Hill Education, 2005.

Spike Milligan, Anthony Clare, *Depression and How to Survive It.* Ebury Press, 1993.

The internet as a source of further information

After reading this book, you may feel that you would like further information on the subject. The internet is of course an excellent place to look and there are many websites with useful information about medical disorders, related charities and support groups.

It should always be remembered, however, that the internet is unregulated and anyone is free to set up a website and add information to it. Many websites offer impartial advice and information that have been compiled and checked by qualified medical professionals. Some, on the other hand, are run by commercial organisations with the purpose of promoting their own products. Others still are run by pressure groups, some of which will provide carefully assessed and accurate information whereas others may be suggesting medications or treatments that are not supported by the medical and scientific community.

Unless you know the address of the website you want to visit – for example, www.familydoctor.co.uk – you may find the following guidelines useful when searching the internet for information.

Search engines and other searchable sites

Google (www.google.co.uk) is the most popular search engine used in the UK, followed by Yahoo! (http://uk.yahoo.com) and MSN (www.msn.co.uk). Also popular are the search engines provided by Internet Service Providers such as Tiscali and other sites such as the BBC site (www.bbc.co.uk).

In addition to the search engines that index the whole web, there are also medical sites with search facilities, which act almost like mini-search engines, but cover only medical topics or even a particular area of medicine. Again, it is wise to look at who is responsible for compiling the information offered to ensure that it is impartial and medically accurate. The NHS Direct site (www.nhsdirect. nhs.uk) is an example of a searchable medical site.

Links to many British medical charities can be found at the Association of Medical Research Charities' website (www.amrc.org.uk) and at Charity Choice (www.charitychoice.co.uk).

Search phrases

Be specific when entering a search phrase. Searching for information on 'cancer' will return results for many different types of cancer as well as on cancer in general. You may even find sites offering astrological information. More useful results will be returned by using search phrases such as 'lung cancer' and 'treatments for lung cancer'. Both Google and Yahoo! offer an advanced search option that includes the ability to search for the exact phrase; enclosing the search phrase in quotes, that is, 'treatments for lung cancer', will have the same effect. Limiting a search to an exact phrase reduces the number of results returned but it is best to refine a search to an exact match only if you are not getting useful results with a normal search. Adding 'UK' to your search term will bring up mainly British sites, so a good phrase might be 'lung cancer' UK (don't include UK within the quotes).

Always remember that the internet is international and unregulated. It holds a wealth of valuable information but individual sites may be biased, out of date or just plain wrong. Family Doctor Publications accepts no responsibility for the content of links published in this series.

Index

Your pages

We have included the following pages because they may help you manage your illness or condition and its treatment.

Before an appointment with a health professional, it can be useful to write down a short list of questions of things that you do not understand, so that you can make sure that you do not forget anything.

Some of the sections may not be relevant to your circumstances.

We are always pleased to receive constructive criticism or suggestions about how to improve the books. You can contact us at:

Email: familydoctor@btinternet.com
Letter: Family Doctor Publications
         PO Box 4664
         Poole
         BH15 1NN

Thank you

Health-care contact details

Name:

Job title:

Place of work:

Tel:

Name:

Job title:

Place of work:

Tel:

Name:

Job title:

Place of work:

Tel:

Name:

Job title:

Place of work:

Tel:

Significant past health events – illnesses/
operations/investigations/treatments

Event	Month	Year	Age (at time)

Appointments for health care

Name:

Place:

Date:

Time:

Tel:

Name:

Place:

Date:

Time:

Tel:

Name:

Place:

Date:

Time:

Tel:

Name:

Place:

Date:

Time:

Tel:

Appointments for health care

Name:

Place:

Date:

Time:

Tel:

Name:

Place:

Date:

Time:

Tel:

Name:

Place:

Date:

Time:

Tel:

Name:

Place:

Date:

Time:

Tel:

Current medication(s) prescribed by your doctor

Medicine name:

Purpose:

Frequency & dose:

Start date:

End date:

Medicine name:

Purpose:

Frequency & dose:

Start date:

End date:

Medicine name:

Purpose:

Frequency & dose:

Start date:

End date:

Medicine name:

Purpose:

Frequency & dose:

Start date:

End date:

Other medicines/supplements you are taking, not prescribed by your doctor

Medicine/treatment:

Purpose:

Frequency & dose:

Start date:

End date:

Medicine/treatment:

Purpose:

Frequency & dose:

Start date:

End date:

Medicine/treatment:

Purpose:

Frequency & dose:

Start date:

End date:

Medicine/treatment:

Purpose:

Frequency & dose:

Start date:

End date:

Questions to ask at appointments
(Note: do bear in mind that doctors work under great time
pressure, so long lists may not be helpful for either of you)

Questions to ask at appointments
(Note: do bear in mind that doctors work under great time pressure, so long lists may not be helpful for either of you)

Notes